FALL OR FLY

FALL OR FLY

The Strangely Hopeful Story of Foster Care
and Adoption in Appalachia

WENDY WELCH

OHIO UNIVERSITY PRESS   ATHENS

Ohio University Press, Athens, Ohio 45701
ohioswallow.com
© 2018 by Wendy Welch

To obtain permission to quote, reprint, or otherwise reproduce or distribute
material from Ohio University Press publications, please contact our rights
and permissions department at (740) 593-1154 or (740) 593-4536 (fax).

Printed in the United States of America
Ohio University Press books are printed on acid-free paper ⊗ ™

27 26 25 24 23 22 21 20 19 18   5 4 3 2 1

Hardcover ISBN: 978-0-8214-2301-1
Paperback ISBN:978-0-8214-2302-8
Electronic ISBN: 978-0-8214-4623-2

Library of Congress Cataloging-in-Publication Data available.
Names: Welch, Wendy, author.
Title: Fall or fly : the strangely hopeful story of foster care and adoption
in Appalachia / Wendy Welch.
Description: Athens, Ohio : Ohio University Press, 2017. | Includes
bibliographical references.
Identifiers: LCCN 2017036216| ISBN 9780821423011 (hardback) | ISBN
9780821423028 (pb) | ISBN 9780821446232 (pdf)
Subjects: LCSH: Adoption--Appalachian Region. | Foster home care--Appalachian
Region. | Social work with children--Appalachian Region. | BISAC: FAMILY &
RELATIONSHIPS / Adoption & Fostering. | SOCIAL SCIENCE / Social Work.
Classification: LCC HV875.56.A7 W45 2017 | DDC 362.73/30974--dc23
LC record available at https://lccn.loc.gov/2017036216

This book is dedicated to the many brave

souls who took time from their lives to tell

their stories—and then went back and

reentered them, day in, day out.

God Bless.

Rock-a-bye baby

In the treetop,

When the wind blows,

The cradle will rock.

When the bough breaks,

The cradle will fall,

And down will come baby,

Cradle and all.

Contents

Acknowledgments

It is impossible to thank the many people who told me their stories here, but please know you're in my thoughts and prayers and some of you are my heroes. Thanks to the early draft readers, particularly Kathy Still and Beth O'Connor, for their insightful comments. Much love to my husband, Jack Beck, for taking on most of the bookstore's needs so I could concentrate on the interviews and writing. And undying gratitude to the anonymous supervisor at a senior level who, when told of this book, said, "It would be wonderful if more people knew about our work. I never want to hear about the project again."

Introduction

Welcome to Coalton

*True, beneath the human façade, I was an interloper, an alien whose
ship had crashed beyond hope of repair in the backwoods of Southern
Appalachia—but at least I'd learned to walk and talk enough like the
locals to be rejected as one of their own.*

—*Sol Luckman*

A baby is born with a need to be loved—and never outgrows it.

—*Frank A. Clark*

THERE ARE two ways to achieve parenthood in this life: sex and paperwork.
Most people prefer the first method, but it's good to know there's something
else to fall back on.

The world of foster care is an amazing place, a maze of a place, a
blazing mess of a place, and one of the most strangely hopeful places
you can enter. Accent on "strange." If you say the words "foster care,"
people's minds fly to the inner city: New York, Chicago, Los Angeles, and
their skyscraping poverty. Add "adoption in Appalachia," and here come

the consanguinity jokes. "Aren't you all one big happy family anyway? Why make it official?"

Investigating foster care and adoption in the Appalachian Coalfields provides little opportunity for laughter, however. The truth is that more than 90 percent of the children up for adoption in this region have living parents.[1] In the majority of cases, the kids are "available" because of their parents' substance abuse, and since dealing drugs tends to be a family business (and using drugs a genetic scourge), these children have no suitable blood relations to look after them.

Perhaps it is best to start with a description rather than with statistics. In the same way that the Ozarks or the West Coast can be both stretched to a one-size-fits-all covering and narrowed to specific zip codes, Appalachia has at least two definitions. The US government says it is a vast stretch of economic, geographic, and population diversity encompassing portions of twelve states from Alabama to New York, plus the whole of West Virginia. In casual usage, "Appalachia" tends to mean the central belt of this governmental stretch, rife with mountains and coal seams. If Appalachia is a beautiful, resilient, misunderstood place, Central Appalachia is its poster child.

Then there are the Coalfields, which are part but not all of Central Appalachia. This mostly mountainous region is—save for a sprinkling of cities—sparsely populated, low on jobs outside the extraction industry, and full of twists and turns in roads and cultural mindset alike. Both physical and mental navigation can be difficult to the newcomer. Also, Coalfields isn't an official term: Are there coal mines nearby? Okay, you're in the Coalfields.

Take West Virginia out of the picture and focus on an area consisting of almost equal parts of Kentucky, North Carolina, Virginia, and Tennessee. Therein sit upward of 12,000 children with living parents who have lost custody—a big number, and every single one of them has a face, a name, a story. Let's pull that unfathomable statistic down again by focusing on a location that is losing its coal and lumber mainstays yet filling up with foster kids, 496 at a recent count. We'll call it Coalton, in honor of its heritage. Coalton spans two states, encompasses one large (50,000+ residents) and a few small (fewer than 5,000 people) cities, and includes parts of the Unaka, Cumberland, and Chilhowee mountain ranges, as well as the Smokies. It is where I conducted the interviews in this book.

Permit me to introduce myself next. I'm an Appalachian born outside Great Rock, a midsized town in Coalton that has been my home for the past decade. These days I own a bookstore and direct a health organization; in my earlier years, I was a journalist and then a professional storyteller. I am neither a foster parent nor a foster child.

WHO'S TELLING THESE STORIES, AND WHY?

In these pages you will meet several social workers, but four are recurring characters: Cody, the hard-talking cynical altruist; sweet, brokenhearted Beth; feisty young Barbie, half righteous indignation, half passionate hope; and wise elder statesman Dale, who has guided them all. They will be your guides for this inquiry, and they are composite characters. Their personalities are based on those of key social workers I came to know well, but the words these characters speak come from many workers interviewed during the year I spent gathering the sixty-two separate oral histories represented in this book. To protect anonymity, and also to frame the inquiry in a way that makes it flow, the social workers are combined into these four, plus a few others.

So when I say that "Dale" asked me to develop this book, I mean that a man with an amazing reputation in his community, backed by colleagues in his agency, e-mailed to ask, "Could you do for foster parents what you did for those cancer patients?"

Two years before, a regional cancer center had offered a grant to help cancer survivors shape their stories into tellable narratives for those not facing the same journey. The storytellers and I then went to various faith and community centers where these survivors, sometimes along with family members who had lost loved ones, told their personal tales to intimate audiences. One of these was the church where Dale serves as pastor. The project resulted in bittersweet tears, exchanged phone numbers, and an increase in appointments at free screening clinics. That last outcome had been the stated goal of the grant.

"Could you do that for foster parenting?" Dale asked. "I think more people would do it [become foster parents] if they understood a few things. Get us some storytellers going. And could you write a book?"

In 2012, St. Martin's Press published my memoir describing the comedic adventures of opening a bookstore in a small Coalfields town. But St. Martin's was a big New York City publisher with major distribution channels; a regional book would not interest them, and the opportunity to feature regional voices was what interested us. Also, as I pointed out to Dale, *Little Bookstore* was about running a bookshop, something I had actually done. My background included neither social work nor foster parenting.

Dale is a very persuasive guy, so we dropped the book idea and altered the live storytelling plan to an online forum. Soon we were plotting access strategies. Social workers tend to be reticent and bound by regulations—and full of untold stories roiling below their calm surface demeanors.

We settled on a regional blog as the venue. *Adoption in Appalachia* would provide anonymity, dignity, and a timeless forum for people who felt ready to tell their stories. It circumvented any potential exploitation of tales that really belonged to children too young to give permission for telling them. Best of all, the stories didn't have to be cleared with "headquarters" because no one would ever know who the social workers were.

That beginning was my first clue of just how deep into the inky blackness of uncharted waters this storytelling journalism project could go. Most reporters will tell you that we are guided by an insatiable curiosity coupled with a willingness to be invasive. As I listened to foster parents, social workers, adopted and foster children, and support-service people like pastors and counselors tell their stories, I began to form questions. Questions that would not go away.

What does it mean to love someone? When is it acceptable to judge someone for how they do something that you're not even willing to try? Who is foster care for, the children or the community around them? How long can this system sustain itself?

With information and support gathering in full swing—and with questions buzzing like angry bees inside me—Dale and I planned to launch the blog at an Appalachian Studies Association Conference held at East Tennessee State University. Shortly after the information on our session went out in the preconference program, an e-mail arrived from Gillian Berchowitz. She had read about our storytelling blog on adoption. Was there a book associated with the project? No? Would we like there to be?

Dale answered his phone on the second ring. I read him the e-mails, then added, "Dude, that was cheating, playing your minister card to ask God for a publisher."

I could hear him grinning all the way down the phone line.

That's how the opportunity to give voice to a group of people who rarely get such a hearing entered our lives. The goal was to make sure the stories were honest: no cotton-candy sweetness or sparkling rainbow veils.[2] But the stories also depended on my access to people willing to talk to me and on how eager they were to tell of their own experiences. As a result, this book has tilts and twirls to it; I make no pretense that this is a comprehensive picture, just that it is a deeply veined one, sometimes hitting seams that have been left embedded without translation from the chaotic vernacular in which they were uncovered. If the stories told here don't seem to make sense sometimes, or seem like they shouldn't have happened, that's because they don't make sense and probably shouldn't have happened.

Gillian was particularly interested in a book that focused on the true day-to-day tales of those inside this localized world of adoption and foster care. Thus, these stories had to deal in a fair but unequivocal manner with the years of exploitation that the mass media have laid over people's understandings of Central Appalachia. No poverty stereotypes, no easy applications of "everybody knows," and no apologies for not being inspirational. Although the work encompasses cultural issues that may be unique to Appalachia, the stories offer little comparison between Coalton and the rest of the country, citing only a few statistics to show how Coalfields residents stack up against the wider world. Comparisons and statistics are for the most part restricted to the endnotes.

Since you were interested enough to pick up a book on the subject, likely you already understand that foster care is an international issue with significant cultural variations. *Fall or Fly* examines small areas of a defined multistate region within a single country. While foster care in Coalton may differ from or bear burdens similar to how foster care functions and dysfunctions in other places, this inquiry is about a few places inside the Coalfields, representing the larger picture.

I said "no apologies," but perhaps one is owed to Dale, who started this project in order to recruit foster parents. The more people inside this world talked, the deeper their stories became—and the more I worried that what had been intended as recruitment had morphed into exposé. Social workers are rarely given a free pass to tell tales, so it's only natural that the negative stories came first; the reader should keep this in mind and try not to build a false picture if many of the events narrated here showcase frustration rather than inspiration. It's good that the project offered social workers a chance to tell their side, because foster care stories are like twelve-sided dice: you never know what's coming up, depending on who's doing the telling.

As for Dale, he let me off the hook one day while I struggled to articulate how few of the stories held "commercially viable" inspirational appeal.

"We don't want to recruit under false pretenses, and we don't want parents who think they'll be the next Hallmark movie. Just tell the stories truthfully. That's enough."

I hope so, because *Fall or Fly* encompasses humans full of rage and a system plagued by crazy, alongside homes redolent with warmth and offering pathways to possibility. The takeaway most will find here has two parts:

1. Adopted and foster children, their parents, and their social workers include some of the most hopeful humans you will ever meet.

2. Despite official-speak, they have had few reasons and even less encouragement to be so hopeful.

Children in Coalton's foster care system are doubly burdened. First, they're kids. Who listens to kids, even when they're trying to articulate their own needs in the face of harsh circumstances? Second, those from Appalachia's Coalfields have grown accustomed to being helped rather than listened to. History has taught citizens here that helpers aren't interested in what we people of Appalachia know, far less in who we know ourselves to be; they're here to "fix" us so we can be all they know we can be, if only we knew better. That applies to kids too.

It is undignified to be a victim. The Coalfields population may or may not be one; answers vary with each person you might gather the courage to ask. But these young'uns shifting between houses with no say in the matter, learning contradictory rules with each move, bleeding dignity every time they stuff their personal belongings into a garbage bag and occupy the backseat of a car? They are victimized. Self-efficacy is the first casualty, followed by trust, confidence, hope, and a viable future. Yet these children are our future.

COLLECTING THE STORIES

The interviews resumed after Dale's encouragement, this time more in-depth, taking little diamonds of individual telling and turning them into as holistic as possible a depiction of what's going on in foster care and adoption in the Coalfields. Phone calls and "I can meet you at the Mountainside Dairy Queen tomorrow morning" notes flew via Facebook Messenger. The core group of a dozen people who'd been my informant base expanded, slowly, as trust built.

We—the social workers, the foster kids, and I—were careful in the telling and collection of stories. Nobody's real name appears in any of the transcripts; I kept forgetting real names and called informants by their pseudonyms when asking for follow-up interviews, causing moments of confused merriment. When possible, interviewees read the drafts of their stories and made tweaks or comments. In the early stages, not many foster parents were willing to speak to me, so I worried about balance when social workers and foster kids discussed events involving foster families. Yet both groups also willingly told uncomplimentary stories about themselves.

The first in line to talk tended to be the social workers. Former and current foster children were a mixed bag of reluctance and eagerness; foster parents rarely returned phone calls; adoptive parents were mostly happy to chat; but it was the social workers who loosed pent-up torrents that turned mountain stoicism into volcanoes spitting boiling lava.

Social workers and foster parents have several things in common, and the first one you notice, when standing outside listening in, is that neither group can catch a break in public opinion. They are either saints or sinners—"no middle ground," as one interviewee said months later, articulating the observation in a single phrase. Foster parents tend to be seen either as naïve victims for taking a cuckoo's egg into their nest or as paragons like Mother Theresa. Either way, bless your heart but you're not to be trusted, because you're not like the rest of us humans.

As for the public's opinion of social workers, who would do that job for that pay? Their very altruism made them suspect. Social workers rarely get to talk without repercussions, and they really wanted people to understand that Coalton culture sometimes eats social programs for lunch. Over and over again, the stories social workers told hit a common theme: parents who were part of the problem rather than the solution. It took a lot of listening to get past the anger and hear the reasons behind the stories the workers wanted to tell. Social workers in the Coalfields vary widely in type and temperament, but if I had to choose one phrase with which to summarize their perspective, it would be "benevolent frustration."

One of my earliest lessons in listening with discernment during conversations between foster parents and social workers came from asking the latter about things they didn't deal with directly. (I asked about group homes.) Caseworkers who had been talking nonstop at one hundred words per minute shut down faster than a flooded coal mine. And proved harder to open back up. Finally, it became clear: what dedicated social workers couldn't change for the better, they wouldn't talk about. That thing did not exist in their world. Cut off the part you can't save; close the doors on the energy drain that won't yield results. Eventually, I learned that this defense mechanism applied equally to government bureaucracy, bad foster parents, and kids who were their own worst enemies.

What's interesting in light of this observation is that the workers talked practically nonstop about foster parents overly concerned with money or morals. If you think about it, maybe that's a hopeful sign. Because social workers don't waste their breath on things they can't change, if the bulk of their venting centered on foster parents, then foster parenting is likely a place where awareness can bring about positive change. I'd like to think so, given that my original intent was to recruit foster parents.

Interviews with foster parents proved more difficult. Social workers thrust contact details on me with the parents' permission, but the latter often exhibited passive resistance when I called. Too busy, so sorry. Actual refusals varied in wording but centered on the foster parents' feeling that they had little good to say about the system, coupled with reluctance to discourage someone considering being a foster parent. Some felt their experiences were too stereotypical to be understood outside the region. Others thought them too unique to avoid identification; they didn't want to be targeted, prosecuted, or recognized. Four interviewees or contacted individuals narrated similar tales of coping with an older foster's inappropriate behavior to a younger child yet forbade publishing that story because people would recognize them.

Adoptive parents, on the other hand, were eager to talk. Most started as foster parents and fell in love with specific children. They were as happy to relate their history as any couple explaining how they met and fell in love. Adoptive parents were also more forthcoming about existing and prior struggles with their children. When I first mentioned the different trust levels observed between foster and adoptive parents during interviews, I was standing in the office parking lot after meeting with Cody about how to proceed in collecting stories. He said he wasn't surprised and offered an early clue into the difference between adoption and foster care, as viewed by case managers (those who oversee the care of displaced children). He suggested that most people doing foster care for good reasons wind up adopting.

"Long-term foster homes are where you find the stuff going on that you don't want to find. Not always, but our goal is always adoption." Parents who foster, unless they do respite or emergency care, tend to wind up realizing that the best way to make a difference is to choose one child or sibling group and adopt. "So you're trying to talk to those who are feeling too new to talk, or maybe they're not wanting a lot of disclosure. Or they're trying to adopt and getting yanked around by the bio parents and the system. Either way, they're in limbo."

At the time, barely two weeks into the interviews, his comment didn't resonate. I watched Cody hop into his jeep, scribbled his words on the back of a napkin in my car (fieldworkers take note: never turn your recorder off, even in the parking lot after a good night's collecting), and filed the comment under "see if this attaches to something later." A month later, what he'd meant made sense. You'll read in this book several narratives of people who made the journey through foster care to adoption.

Then there were the interviews with kids. We set ground rules: No one under the age of fifteen. Aged-out adults who used to be in foster families were preferred. I could make observations while attending family-fun events held by Department of Social Services (DSS) or therapeutic agencies but could not conduct interviews. In the end, I talked to nine foster kids, past and present. They were the smallest group of interviewees.

WHO ARE THESE STORIES FOR?

Like foster parents and social workers, Appalachia is a sitting duck for judgment from people who watch life there unfold in dysfunctional hi-def from the coziness of an armchair. In Coalton, blaming the victim and suspecting those who came to help have both been elevated to art forms. If this book produces mission-like zeal toward adopting children out of Appalachia, as a couple of child advocates from outside Coalton have suggested it should, then *Fall or Fly* will have failed. The last time a wave of do-gooders swooped in to rescue children from communities deemed unfit to raise them? Ask your nearest Native American friend how that worked out.

First and foremost, this work intends to honor social workers. Their words shape its core. If honesty about what they face every day comes across as negativity, let that vented anger stand as its own tribute to those who expressed it. God bless any woman trying to make life better for children she did not bear, and any man who did not biologically father the child he seeks to help.

But this book also seeks to offer appreciation where blame-the-victim mentalities run rampant, such as with the urban poor or in ethnically cohesive communities, as well as in the Coalfields of Appalachia. If you're from a place targeted by other people trying to tell you what you're supposed to be and why you aren't up to that benchmark, please hear this message: the problems within a community are not only solved by those who live in that community but also should be defined by that community. We who live with the problems know when something works and when it doesn't and where priorities need to lie.

This book is dedicated with love and respect to Coalton's residents, especially those who were or are foster children. I hope it answers questions for anyone who has asked, "I wonder what it would be like to foster a child?" Foster parenting is tricky, yet you might be the only chance some children will ever find, the sole source of stability and affection they will come to believe in or learn from. Herein lie depictions of how several parents, children, and social workers felt about their ride on that bucking bronco. It is for you to decide what role, if any, you might play in this rodeo. (P.S.: Dale would like to hear from you if you decide you're interested.)

WRITING OTHER PEOPLE'S STORIES

Coalton is a small place made up mostly of tiny towns and rural municipalities, so the stories told here have been scrambled to protect the identities of the tellers. All of them are true, but I've rearranged where they happened, to whom, and when so as to render the main characters invisible where they live. Secrets shared here are often "open" ones—meaning that everyone knows, but no one names names. Scrambling ensures that those who spoke with brave honesty aren't rewarded with public criticism.[3] As one participant put it, "Everyone dealing with the foster care and adoption world should get cut a little slack."

Speaking of slack-cutting, the writing style in this nonfiction work is called storytelling journalism for several reasons. Although as a former journalist I wanted quotes to be the exact words of the interviewee, I removed distinguishing speech characteristics such as repeated profanity, dialect, colloquial grammar, and verbal tics. In the few instances when interviews were not digitally recorded, quotations fleshed out from notes were rendered as accurately as possible. If a pseudonym was assigned and the person used a real name, the pseudonym has been substituted without brackets. This also applies to place names, all of which are fake. Descriptions are of the real locations.

Interviewees participated firsthand in the events they described to me; barring a few exceptions, I was never present at those events. In some cases, I could approach others involved for corroboration; sometimes trust deepened, and return interviews closed holes in the patchwork of the first telling. When that happened, the events may sound as if I'd been standing there. But sometimes there was no way to get more detail. Circumstances varied. If the story reads more like journalism, quoting one person, it's because there was no way to reach deeper than a single source.

And while it may seem odd to put a conclusion in the opening of a book, permit me to summarize with (or introduce, if you prefer) five words that will resonate throughout the interviews, stories, and thoughts that describe adoption and foster care in Coalton: Chaos. Frustration. Compassion. Desperation. Hope. You will hear echoes of these words as you read, and we will return to them near the end of the book.

Read it and laugh. Read it and weep. Read it with one of my favorite Dr. Seuss quotes in mind: "Unless someone like you cares a whole awful lot, nothing is going to get better. It's not."

1

Looking for Love—and Babies

We tried IVF. No luck. We discussed adoption, researched, found lots of very expensive ways, and some exotic ones. We did not have big bucks to spend, plus heard horror stories of highly paid attorneys selling babies, which later had to be returned. Sounded scary. We checked out Chinese adoption; we had friends who did that successfully. Only cost about $4,000. We could swing that. Signed up, had an extensive home study, then we waited and waited. After spending about $1,500 and waiting more than a year, we received a letter telling us the wait was going to be years longer than first advised. We were distraught.

Out of the blue a few weeks later, we got a late-night phone call from my wife's parents. A friend of theirs who had heard casually that we were looking to adopt was a social worker at a hospital in a neighboring town. A college student had shown up about to deliver just before Christmas. Her parents did not know of the pregnancy, and the girl wanted to finish college before starting a family. She said if the social worker could have the baby in a good home by Christmas, she would give the child up for adoption. The home must be with parents of good repute who were educated and immediately available.

All of this we learned at 11:00 p.m. Our attorney was in the hospital with documents for the girl to sign at 8:30 the next morning, and the agreement was made. Our daughter was in our arms thirty-six hours after we learned of her existence.

—adopting dad

PEOPLE BECOME foster parents for a surprisingly small number of reasons that tend to fall into a handful of broad patterns: couples who are unable to have children of their own; empty nesters who want to do the whole parenting cycle again; those who want to do good in the world; and people interested in money, free labor, or other things besides the best interests of the children they take in.

Although that last group hogs quite a bit of bandwidth in the public's perception, social workers unite in saying that first among equals are the couples unable to conceive. In many parts of America, childless hopefuls look not only to costly infertility treatments (such as in vitro fertilization [IVF]) but beyond the country's borders. Russian orphans and baby girls from China head this list in American public awareness, but IVF and international adoptions are rare in Coalton, mostly because both require serious cash. Coalton's people tend to be poorer than the average working-class person, the bulk of salaries hovering at around 120 percent of poverty level,[1] except in University City. Costly paths to becoming a parent are out.

This includes third-party domestic private adoptions, which can be expensive and explosive to navigate. "Third-party" here means outside of one's extended family; a woman's adopting her sister's children is not a third-party adoption. Domestic adoption inquiries are the first crossroads where Dale's hopes meet those of infertile couples because fostering a child can place you first in line to adopt. The difficulty of getting information out to people, not to mention the understandable fact that most couples want infants, is the main factor that seems to stymie the process of getting children without homes into homes without children.

"People who can't have kids go into the system until they find the children that fit what makes them feel like a family, and then they adopt them and get out," says Beth, a former social worker who left after five years on the job. "But they go in looking for babies, so they either wait a long time, or they fall in love with an older child they foster while they're waiting."

Beth works now as a legal secretary in sleepy little Riverside, a town of about two thousand residents where Main Street boasts more lawyers and hairdressers than retail shops. Historic buildings sit empty or have pop-up thrift stores spread in their showcase windows. Behind the row of nineteenth-century buildings sits an ancient mountain wall, bright green in the spring, powdered white in winter. Beth and I saw both as we met week after week in a family-owned bakery on one corner.

Beth suggested that location because she could walk to it from her office and got only an hour for lunches. The first time I walked into the bakery, the large sign on the back wall caught my attention: "Families are like fudge— mostly sweet with a few nuts."

She laughed when I pointed out the sign to her. "I never thought of that being portentous. I like their salads."

Beth reiterated that she was participating in the interviews because of Dale's desire to recruit foster parents. She thought it important to get out the word that foster kids may be eligible for a modest-to-significant stipend through a legitimate state agency, something the general public doesn't always grasp. Not only do prospective fosters and adopters not pay service fees in state adoptions, they might also receive financial help for the child's care. The amount depends on the child's age and needs. The needs classification that Beth worked with most often was "therapeutic." This means the child has special needs, usually based on medical fragility, developmental delays, or the behavioral health effects of long-term bouncing through the system. Therapeutic designations can raise monthly support to as much as three times what a child without one would receive; for teenagers, the monthly therapeutic stipend would be $1,800, as compared to $671 for teens not considered to have the same needs.

It's one of those ideas that looks good on paper, Beth added, but a discerning reader can see quickly where inappropriate attraction might occur. The stipends pay more for people to keep "undesirable" kids who are considered less adoptable, in hopes that the foster parents will fall in love with that troublesome young'un as time goes by. People fostering because they can't have children of their own want babies, or at least kids under six, but they also want to love someone. Sometimes they do fall in love with an older kid while waiting for a younger one to become available.

That's what happened with Abby and her husband, John, people Beth suggested I talk to. Abby agreed to meet me at my bookstore in Great Rock and tell her story.

She and John married at age eighteen for her, nineteen for him, in a little wooden mountain church with a steeple, full of friends and flowers. Let's call their sprawled-out hamlet of eight hundred residents Valleyfield, since it climbs the slope of one of the prettiest valleys in Coalton. Excited at the prospect of a family Abby fully intended would bloom with a new child every other year, she miscarried twins thirteen months later. Her family doctor told her after a barrage of tests that she would be lucky ever to carry a baby full-term.

A haze of confusion and questions followed. Devout Christians, Abby and John wondered if her condition were a test from God of their faith, and if they just needed to believe He would send them a child after all. Or could something be done medically? The undercurrents of Abby's physician's warning tugged at their plans: it wasn't impossible for her to conceive; it was dangerous. And if she could give birth, the infant would probably have significant health issues.

The young couple went numb. Abby heard the voices of family and friends, the prayers of her community, and her own frantic thoughts as a long tunnel of words and sounds, far removed yet claustrophobic, encasing her in noise. From this miasma a few voices emerged with clarity, those of friends at church who told them about foster care.

Those friends probably said several things then, but John and Abby heard one specific and succinct message: fostering would be the quickest way to adoption. That began to feel like a combination of their last hope and Divine Guidance.

Abby and John moved from tiny Valleyfield to Walker City (population 3,500) where John's career prospects improved. They didn't it know yet, but that relocation probably also increased their chances of fostering. Valleyfield's ancient water and sewage systems contained lead pipes, straight pipes, and suspect wells. Other would-be foster families in towns similar to Valleyfield had seen their foster home applications rejected over water quality.

The requirements for fostering include far more than good sewage systems. Abby and John underwent a psychological profile and answered personal questions about their finances, marriage, and mental-health backgrounds. They submitted to a criminal background check. They had blood tests (to rule out tuberculosis and HIV). And they attended night classes in CPR, blood-borne pathogens, and parenting. Another home visit ensured they knew how to work their fire extinguisher and didn't have any porn magazines lying around, among other things. The inspectors measured the crib-slat widths because the couple had asked about getting an infant, and the bedrooms' dimensions because they'd agreed to take more than one child at a time.

"It was invasive. We didn't have anything to hide, but it still felt like getting turned inside out," Abby recalls. "We knew it was important, and it wasn't personal; but some stranger sits asking you questions about your husband, you're going to get antsy."

Eventually, all those tests turned into the piece of paper they coveted: a license to be foster parents. Abby left her job to stay home and wait, and soon the phone rang. They took in boys and girls, babies and ten-year-olds in rapid succession, most being what is called "temporary placement" kids—that is, children who need a safe place for a time but aren't available for adoption. The few who were available didn't seem to fit John and Abby's home style.

"We weren't being picky, but you know what you know. We believed in God's guidance."

About two years after they'd begun fostering, the call that would change their lives came. Standing in her kitchen, Abby listened to a disembodied voice on the other end of the line describe half sisters, one seven, one nine, victims of parental drug abuse and neglect. They had been at an emergency foster home for a few days because Birth Mom's rights were going to be terminated by court order. It had taken a little longer than anticipated, so the girls needed a foster home prepared to house them for a month or two. After that they would be up for adoption.

Looking back, Abby says, "We had calls asking us to take kids all the time, some short-term, some long-term. All I can say is this one had electricity running through it. Like it was meant."

But it started in the same way the others did. As in previous cases, the social worker needed an immediate response regarding the home's availability. "You do all this careful planning, all your praying, mounds of paperwork, and then none of that matters. When it really happens and they need you, there isn't even time to think. There wasn't time to call my husband, just say yes or no on the phone, and that was it."

While she was driving to pick up the girls, Abby's thoughts were consumed by the fact that this would be the sisters' second move within the week. The product of a loving, stable extended family, Abby longed to give all her foster kids that same experience she had had, but for some reason, this pair had gone straight to her heart.

"I think I was in love with them before I even saw them," she says in hindsight. "I'd fostered before, but this felt different."

Different though it may have felt, the two redheaded girls who waited, clutching black trash bags—the luggage of choice for foster kids—looked scared, just like the others. All eyes and legs and cautious stares, they wore shorts, ill-fitting tank tops, and flip-flops in late October. *Shy,* Abby thought. *Why wouldn't they be? Two homes in one week?*

What Abby didn't learn for months, until the sisters began to open up and tell their stories, was that she and John were their ninth foster home within three years. At that moment, she swore to God that those frightened little girls would receive the stability they'd been lacking. Guidance, care, and safety would blossom into love.

Which it did. Abby and John told the girls they'd be adopting them and started the process—until Bio Mom appeared suddenly with a court order saying that the girls had to be returned to her. Again. She had stopped their adoptions before, getting clean and taking the children home, only to lose them within the year. That was why the girls had bounced so much over the past three years.

Nothing had ever felt so wrong before, this edict that their foster daughters had to go home with Bio Mom. Abby and John had returned kids to bad situations in the past, amid prayers and tears, but this time they sought legal help. When every avenue and their bank account were exhausted, they tried to explain to the girls that this return was neither their idea nor their fault. But what the sisters heard was that they were going to live with Mom again—even though they did not want to. As foster kids often do, these girls, particularly the older one, knew that if they went back, it was just a matter of time until they would leave again.

"'And the next place might not be like you. Please don't let them take us back.'" Abby's voice takes on a childlike pleading and a shaky edge as she quotes the older girl. "You don't know heartbreak until you look into innocent blue eyes like that and say, 'I'm sorry; we did everything we could, but we can't keep you.' And they heard everything you said, but they're just babies, and they ask why you don't want them anymore; did they do something wrong?"

When she says, "Everything we could," Abby means it. The couple considered legal and illegal plans, yet in the end there was nothing plausible to do but to obey the law and return the red-haired sisters they had hoped would be their daughters.

It is not uncommon for birth parents to swing into action when notification of a pending adoption—which perforce includes termination of both parents' rights—reaches them, says Dale, a social worker with forty-two years of experience.

"The act of adopting disturbs the status quo and moves people in strange ways—birth moms, grandparents, everybody. They come out swinging at the last minute over children who have been floating through the system for years. You can see them holding onto their last chance to get their kids back, or trying to extort a better deal, or maybe exerting that contrary side of human nature we all have. Whatever the reason, it's common."

"Get used to it," Abby advises foster parents seeking to adopt. "There aren't any rules in this game of human hearts. If we could have adopted those girls right then and there, the first time I saw them, I would have. If we could have made it to Canada, we might be living there now."[2]

Heartbroken, the couple took a hiatus, then returned to fostering. Following seven months of bed rest, with "the congregations of three churches holding me up with their prayers," Abby also gave birth to a healthy baby boy. He has an older and younger sibling by adoption.

"God's timing is perfect. He brought me the right children at the right time," Abby says, cuddling her youngest in my bookstore's armchair as he plays with a pop-up book. Born with developmental delays and lifelong medical fragility because of his birth mother's drug habit, he fostered with Abby and John from the age of six months. Again, the social worker placing him told them that he would be adoptable within the year.

Abby snorts, then sighs. "The whole time, I was on tenterhooks inside. Would they let it go through? Would the birth father appear from nowhere? Would it really happen this time?"

It did. At the age of two, he became theirs.

The birth parents' substance abuse is the primary reason most children are in Coalton's foster care system; substance addiction is also the biggest source of that push-me/pull-me stress as to whether children will become adoptable. Before adoption can occur, the birth parents' parental rights need to be terminated. But though they are addicts, they do love their children and often go through multiple cycles of getting "clean," petitioning for the return of their children, staying sober for a time, relapsing into addiction, and losing their children again. Termination of parental rights is meant to be a process of months, but it can actually take years.[3]

Voluntary termination is, of course, faster than involuntary. In his late twenties when interviewed, Hutton was adopted in infancy because he was in the right place—his mother's womb—at the wrong time—her sophomore year of university in Coalton's largest city. Hutton's bio mom got in touch with DSS, and soon after his birth, a couple who'd been on the waiting list for an infant (and had checked the box "either" rather than "boy" or "girl") became his foster parents. Even with Birth Mom on board for a swift, formal termination of her parental rights, the process still took six months.

An older couple with a comfortable income and a suburban home, Hutton's parents weren't interested in fostering; uppermost in their minds were tales from friends who'd fostered, horror stories similar to Abby and John's, of court-ordered returns halfway to adoption or midnight pickups of frightened children. Hutton's mom and dad had also had friends take in kids with special needs that the new parents felt insufficiently trained to meet. As Dale often says, such tales are rampant in the public's perception of fostering, with or without good reason.

Hutton's mom and dad wanted to start clean with an infant who would have no chance of being yanked from their home, so they waited for a baby whose mother was ready to sign off then and there; they were not interested in whether they'd receive a stipend for their newborn because he'd been their foster child first. Most healthy infants don't receive state support, at least not for long; drug-free babies available for immediate adoption are rare, yet what most childless couples start off wanting. Private agencies charge fees just to let parents know such an infant has become available. (When anyone contracted with a state agency or working for DSS does so and gets caught, that's a different matter.)

Hutton's mom, a teacher, and dad, a lab technician, jumped to the head of a queue because money changed hands. This fast track is not open to everyone in Coalton. Would-be parents in Coalton who can find a way to be first when a baby is up for immediate adoption will do so; often this involves personal connections rather than money, as was the case in the story that opens this chapter. Those who can't get to the top of the list by using these means can do so by fostering, while praying for adoption to become a quick option.

Hutton's delighted parents conceived four years later, presenting him with a little brother. The boys grew up on the outskirts of the city where Hutton's mom graduated from university, surrounded by brick houses and professional families who knew Hutton was adopted. Did that affect the family dynamic, internally or in the minds of the community? Hutton considers the question carefully before answering.

"Not the community, no. I mean, our church, our neighbors, everybody knew I was adopted. We lived in the suburbs, so it was no big deal. There were several other kids around me who were adopted. I wasn't some anomaly challenging the social order, so to speak."

Internal to the family, it wasn't so much that being adopted didn't make a difference as that the brothers didn't care that it did, or allow it to. Dad was Dad. Mom found it harder not to favor the bio brother, but now that the boys are fathers to their own families, "We laugh about it when it's just us. Yes, there's a difference; we just don't care that there's a difference."

As Hutton comments about growing up in the suburbs, he nods to his wife, Kim, who is sitting next to him in the bookstore while he tells his story. Kim is also adopted, but her childhood spent growing up in a back hollow of Coalton was very different from Hutton's—and the next chapter in the larger story of adoptions in Coalfields Appalachia.

2

A Different Kind of Love Than I Wanted

Deep down, part of me always wanted to adopt. Watching my son grow up alone because we couldn't have any more, it crossed my mind a lot. One day my wife said, "A friend is looking for someone to adopt her grandbaby because her son is in prison for fifteen years and the baby's mom doesn't want him at all."

In my mind were fears like: Oh, they will get our hopes up and then change their minds, and there will be nothing but trouble the whole eighteen years from the biological parents, and I guess there's no such scenario as a normal couple just wanting to give up a baby from an accidental pregnancy.

But word came that the dad wanted us to have this baby because he couldn't take care of it, and the mom was a wild child living the fast life. She used drugs, and she just didn't want the baby. It was Super Bowl night when we got a call that said she was going into labor. We threw a few clothes together and hit the road. I got to hold him soon after he was born. He was screaming his head off—little did I know that would be a way of life—but what I most remember was how bright pink he was. I thought, "The pink panther!"

I was so excited to hold him but still really cautious of getting attached for fear of the mom changing her mind. She actually was holding him and feeding him quite often. I remember seeing that and thinking, I knew this was too good to be true! She is going to change her mind!

But she didn't, thankfully. I had a lawyer there with the legal papers.
If we hadn't been there, Social Services would have taken him due to the
drugs. When our son was born, they found in her system THC (which is
Pot), Meth, Cocaine, and LSD. And that's how I got my son.

—*adoption dad*

THE ROAD from fostering to adoption can be an arduous journey. It's not
surprising that some find the yo-yo activity of courtroom appearances and
parental-rights visits excruciating and hunt for ways around it, as Hutton's
parents did. Others have that decision thrust upon them.

While Coalton isn't big on expensive private adoptions, it has a fast-
track equivalent often found in rural areas: the hand-picked mom.[1] These
private-but-mostly-unpaid transactions stem from parents who know they
won't be allowed (or don't want) to keep their babies; often the birth mom
or her mother will choose someone they know to raise the infant in question. Based on interviews, the most common reasons for a birth mom's
willingness to give up her child here in Coalton are substance abuse and
illness—usually cancer. In third place comes Mom's need to finish college,
and behind that, her new boyfriend's refusing to raise another man's kid.
Children caught in the crossfire of this last situation are more often of
elementary-school age than infants.

Being singled out for such an honor-cum-responsibility as raising your
blood relation's child pretty much bypasses the state system's fostering plan
and goes straight to "adopt," yet it is fraught with social peril. The new
parents may wind up entangled in a long-term and ill-defined relationship
with people they probably know well and see on weekends—at church
or in the local elementary school, since these adoptions are often in rural
communities. While moms seeking a good parent usually turn first to their
own sisters, mothers, or mothers-in-law, they don't have to. Mom may also
not be the one pulling the decision strings.

Appropriate relatives asked to take the baby may be eligible for assistance under KinCare. This program goes under different names in different
states, but it's the DSS family-first plan. Extended family foster the child
while Mom (or sometimes Dad) gets it together. During this time, the

child is not eligible for adoption. If Mom doesn't mention members of her extended family when her children are taken, social workers try to track them down. Relatives who wind up overlooked during that hunt are eligible to bring litigation when termination of rights comes up, so it's in the best interest of the state to find them if Mom doesn't offer names.

One of the reasons that handpicked adoptions can get messy is their degree of informality. Another is how much harder it becomes to push a birth mom away or curtail her rights by court order when she's the one who gave you the child. Coalton is a region fueled by a dying coal industry and a thriving kinship system, a place where at least some of the extended family are likely to live in the same vicinity. Coal isn't king here; family is. A judge may say it's okay for you not to let the bio mom see her child once she's signed him over to you, but the community never will. And if the community includes her extended family, which it probably does, God help you when you bump into one of the home team at the gas station or grocery store, because they're going to say something. Probably in a carrying tone of voice.

Hutton's wife, Kim, was adopted by her birth mother's boyfriend's sister. Birth mother Kristin moved in with a guy—call him Jim—who didn't want another man's kids. Kristin "gave" her oldest daughter, Janice, to her grandmother and three-year-old Kim to Jim's sister, Annette. (Annette and her husband would have taken Janice as well, but she had a different dad, and he wouldn't let anyone but his former wife's mother have her.) Kim's dad was nowhere to be found, so boyfriend Jim signed the termination papers as her bio father. Which probably made the whole adoption illegal, but who was watching?

Appalachian kinship systems are complex, but Kim's adoption staggered even the clan within which it happened; the whole extended family on both sides lived within twenty miles of one another in a community sprawled across a back holler (the regional term for a mountain hollow, or cove). Kim and Janice even attended the same church as their birth mom for a while—until Kim grew old enough to ask questions. Kim grew up knowing that her sister lived nearby but never got together with her outside of church, which she stopped attending when she was "maybe five or six."

To avoid confusion, references to Kim's mom from here forward mean Annette, her aunt-by-marriage. (Jim and Kristin married a few years later.)

Her birth mother will be called Kristin. The arrangement between the two women was a handshake; Annette received no money via KinCare. The formal adoption flew through uncontested; use of the legal system remained minimal, or someone might have cried foul on Jim's signature as birth dad and questioned the "agreement" Annette and Kristin drew up regarding visitation rights.

Although Kim's mom had signed a document written by Kristin stipulating she could come see Kim on a regular basis, Annette began to find ways to prevent these meetings. Because the agreement was less legal than a gesture of good faith between them, both sisters-in-law stretched its nonbinding language until it broke. Ties were cut by the time Kim started school.

Without a state stipend, her mom sent Kim to the county elementary school in designer clothes, had her hair professionally cut and styled, and enrolled her in dance lessons—which Kim hated. Part of the tension that developed between the women may have stemmed from their different economic classes. Annette's husband, Rick, was career military; Annette was a teacher. For whatever reason, her mom didn't want Kim associating with Kristin and Jim (no fixed source of income) as she grew up.

But Kim had questions and a wound that wouldn't heal. "Why did she want to get rid of me? Why was I not good enough for her? How come she handed me off and ran away? I really, really wanted to know why she gave me up without a fight."

Yearning to know why blotted out the sun in her world, gnawed the strength from her bones, and destroyed her self-identity. Kim managed to keep the anger bottled inside until need met opportunity one winter weekend when she was visiting her grandmother.

Spending a few days with Mamaw was not unusual for Kim if her parents went out of town. Don't confuse Mamaw with Kim's maternal grandmother, who raised her older sister, Janice. The family called that woman Grandma. Mamaw was Annette's mother. As readers have already worked out, that also makes her the mother of Kristin's boyfriend-turned-husband, Jim—the guy who didn't want Kim and her sister around. Such an inconvenient detail not only complicates the story but invites the inbreeding jokes for which Coalton residents have no patience.

It is perhaps easier to turn pain into humor at the expense of others than to consider the implications of Kim's stepfather's sister also being her mother, the stepfather being the reason she couldn't live at home, or his mother's being the babysitter of choice, when Grandma-by-blood sat eight miles away with Kim's older sister, Janice, in her home.

One fateful weekend while staying with Mamaw, Kim just up and asked her to call and see if Kristin and Jim could come over.

"I don't know if Mamaw was surprised. She'd didn't act like it. She'd raised two generations of teenagers [including Jim's daughter from another relationship] by then, so maybe not. Not much phased that woman, I have to say. She just picked up the phone and called them, and they said they'd come over."

Understandably nervous, Kim tried to calm herself: *It's not like you've never seen them before. You've talked to them plenty at funerals and weddings.* But this time, she would be able to ask The Question without extended family hanging about, eavesdropping and reporting back to Annette. Kim knew her mother wouldn't like what was about to happen and didn't want to hurt the woman who had raised her.

Mamaw lived by the side of a two-lane highway that was the main thoroughfare for the holler. On pins and needles while waiting for Kristin, Kim remembers thinking every car that passed might be her mom (Annette), come home early. She feared Mamaw might have called and told Annette what Kim was doing. But she had to know. There was no turning back.

Kristin and Jim lived about six miles away. They entered Mamaw's dark-paneled living room as night was falling, and things started out awkwardly. In the midst of Mamaw's fussing over getting everyone soda and a snack, Kim realized that she couldn't find the nerve to ask. Instead, they sat, Kristin and Jim on the couch, Kim on the piano stool, Mamaw flitting through the room like a butterfly, taking her armchair, rising to the kitchen, and returning. Kim recalls that they "talked, had a few good laughs." As Kim recalls, the closest she came to asking what she really wanted to know was her question "Why don't you ever come see me?"

But she knew the answer before Kristin gave it: Annette didn't want her around. Kim accepted this; the moment passed, and so did the opportunity to ask The Question.

Two years later, Mamaw died, prompting "the funeral of the century. I'm there at the funeral home with my real family, and my bio family is there, every last one of them, including my sister, and my grandma by blood, and this cousin named Dewey, and he was a really nice guy, and you have to remember, I haven't seen any of these people in years. Once Mom found out about that night at Mamaw's, we had us a real crackdown. But my mom is upset that her Mama's dead, and she's all raw inside, and all she sees is me hanging out with the enemy instead of by her side. Please keep in mind I was only twelve. There were a lotta things I didn't get then that I can see now."

Tension mounted. Annette had wanted her daughter to read a poem Annette had written for Mamaw, but when the time came, she told Kim not to trouble herself, stood, and read it in her own breaking voice. From then until Kim left home for good, that funeral became "the festering sore that could not close." The first insult thrown in an argument, the baseline measurement against which everything Kim did wrong as a daughter was pitted, the yardstick for inadequate parenting: Mamaw's funeral.

Kim describes her teenage years as "ups and down, just like any teen and her parents." Options not available to a more traditionally formed family didn't help. When it became difficult to deal with her mom, Kim had "another mother," a woman she didn't think of as Mom but could turn to if she wanted to leave home. Of course, between the normal teen angst and the added weight of "too much family" in a tight geographic space, she inevitably did. One night in the middle of a fight that included the funeral yet again, Kim packed a bag, called Kristin and Jim to inform them that she was on her way, and left.

She stayed two, maybe three weeks in Kristin and Jim's trailer that first time, until her mother came over and begged her to come home. Annette swore things would be different. Kim's dad (Rick) was an alcoholic; he never raised a hand to either of them, but he yelled. A lot. Annette was the classic description of bipolar, although not formally diagnosed. Kim had grown adept over the years at interpreting how her mother's footsteps sounded coming into the kitchen; treads ranging from light to heavy indicated what kind of day Annette was having, and consequently what kind of day Kim and her dad could plan to have.

Kim doesn't feel victimhood or hold grudges about the alcoholism or the bipolarity. "I knew she loved me, and if it was a different kind of love than I wanted, she was still my mom. I went back, but every time we'd get to fighting, I'd pack or she'd up and tell me to pack. It was like the yo-yo from Hell, back and forth up and down the road between the two of them."

Crazy-glue families splintered and put back together in mismatching patterned pieces abound in the rest of the world just as much as in Coalton. Adrian LeBlanc's dissertation-turned-narrative entitled *Random Family* is set in New York City; it's an excellent read on the myriad ways people in big cities create affiliations regardless of DNA's bonds. Paula McLain's memoir *Like Family* describes a similar confusion of foster care life in California. The added burden in places like Kim's back holler is, odds are good that some of your neighbors are part of your crazy-glue family, while others are members of your blood kin. Some are both. Thus the networks of dysfunction are smaller, tighter, and probably sharing the same roads to get to and from most places. You can run; you can hide; but by the time you've settled into your secret refuge, someone in the community has called both your mothers to tell them where you're staying.

In my bookstore hangs a tea towel embroidered with the saying "In a small town, it doesn't matter if you don't know what you're doing, because somebody else does." When Kim and Hutton saw it during her interview, she laughed.

"That," she says, pointing. "That."

Kim left home on extended-family couch-surfing adventures more and more as the years rolled by—not least because she found an ally next door to Kristin's in her maternal grandmother's husband, the man who with his wife had raised Janice (Kim's older sister). Grandpa and Grandma owned the farmhouse whose yard hosted Kristin and Jim's trailer.

"I loved him from the minute I met him. The first time I met him, we were at a birthday party, one of those crazy times with the whole holler there, family, friends, kit and caboodle, and I walked up to him and said, 'I bet you don't know who I am,' and he said, 'Yes, I do, you're my granddaughter Kim.' And I loved him from that minute on."

Kim stayed with Kristin most of the summer between her sophomore and junior years of high school. One afternoon she came out of the house, upset from a phone call with Annette. Grandpa was sitting on the porch, drinking beer. He listened to her tale of woe and then said, "I wish I'd taken you in myself."

Kim started crying.

"It was one of the best conversations I ever had with him, over beer. He loved his beer." Kim's smile speaks volumes as her eyes fill again with tears.

Emphysema took Grandpa the next summer; Kim went home and remained there until two weeks after her eighteenth birthday, during her senior year of high school. Then she moved back in with Jim and Kristin, remaining through graduation. Annette told her husband they would not attend their daughter's ceremony after such a display of ingratitude and disrespect. By this time, Jim was terminally ill, but the man responsible for Kim's leaving home at the age of three came in his wheelchair, Kristin pushing it, to watch Kim graduate.

"Family is weird," Kim says. "That's all."

Kim recognized that more than one rite of passage lay at hand. Her maternal grandmother (widow of her beloved Grandpa) hugged Kim at the graduation party and said, "Now you'll come join us for good." Although she had moved back after her birthday with that intention, Kim felt in the moment of that hug that her decision wasn't just about where she was going to live or who her mother and father "really" were. The time had come to accept or break with the patterns repeating around her. To ignore the community judging Rick for returning early from his stint in Iraq to look after Annette when she contracted cancer. (When he pointed out that Annette couldn't look after their daughter alone while sick, fellow members of his church said, "She's not your daughter. You should've stayed and done your duty.") To reject living like Kristin, who took in and raised her husband Jim's grandson after he had refused to help raise her daughters. Not to be like her sister, Janice, whose oldest child was adopted by his foster family and her second son placed with Kristin after she petitioned the court via KinCare.

"That holler was one big merry-go-round of people taking care of everybody else's kids, and a community acting fit to judge everybody else for it." The generation that didn't raise their own kids wound up raising their grandchildren.

Realizing that "the only way to make money there for a woman was build a meth lab or become a nurse," Kim followed in her father's footsteps and joined the army. Packing in as much travel and education as she could, she made friends with people from very different places, got informally adopted by the family of her best friend in Canada, and turned herself into a stable adult. "It was me or nobody who was going to make that happen. So I did it."

The tension with her mother never resolved. "She was proud of me. My dad was proud of me. But we never really got it together."

After her army stint, Kim returned to the back holler filled with relatives but soon got herself an apartment in Walker City. Her job in a medical office—"Yeah, I did become a nurse, so there," Kim says with a laugh—introduced her to Hutton. Kim was twenty-seven, married, and mother to a little girl when her mom died. Soon after Annette's funeral, she and Hutton left the baby with a friend while they stopped at Food City for groceries. As they shopped, Kim said, "I wonder what Mom will have to say about us leaving Jessie with the neighbors just to run an errand."

Hutton froze, a green pepper in his hand. That's when she remembered.

For an instant, Kim thought, *Dang it, I don't have to worry about what Mom thinks anymore; I'm finally free.* Then she burst into tears in the produce section.

That's what family is like, isn't it? Make jokes about the holler and the complicated mess of Appalachian kinship systems if you will, but one of the most basic relationships on earth still boils down to crying in public because your judgmental mother won't ever yell at you again. It's a little frightening to realize that our deepest interactions and needs reduce to a phrase as simple as that ready-made Facebook relationship status, "It's complicated."

Bio or adopted, welcome to the messy side of family.

3

Through the Eyes of a Child

I still remember the day I knew everything was going to be all right. My foster mom had her [birth] son in the car when she picked me up after school, and they were sick. I mean, they puked, and I don't know what they'd been eating, but the puke was bright orange and really, really disgusting. And I was grossed out at driving home with puke in the car, but I didn't say anything, and sure enough, that night I puked too. My foster dad came and cleaned up my room, twice, when I puked. And I knew then we were family, because nobody had ever, ever cleaned up after me before. You have to really love someone to clean up their puke. Then I knew they loved me and it was going to be all right.

—e-mail from an adopted foster child

"COMPLICATED" MAY describe family at large and the foster care system in detail, but survival within either breaks down to one simple principle for the kids passing through: learn the rules of the house you're going to and abide by them. (And remember that principle's converse: if you're going to break those rules, make it good and final.)

Foster parents tend to view the whole process quite differently, which isn't surprising. Not every foster family's goal is adoption, but the caseworker's ultimate goal is, and most children—even when they say otherwise with crossed arms and belligerent voices—long to be adopted. How often the stated goal influences where a child lands in care is a debatable point. Foster homes may be looking to adopt, providing a temporary service out of compassion, or doing a job for which they feel entitled to payment.

Take a matchmaking service for parents and kids, throw in the love-hate broken promises of bio parents and family, pour money on top, and start the countdown clock. At its most basic level, think from a fifth grader's point of view what it must feel like to enter a house full of strangers when she knows she's being auditioned for the role of daughter. Or when she's one among many residents with no permanent status. Children in a vulnerable frame of mind go to prospective homes on a trial basis—and they know they're losing their cuteness factor with every year that passes after about the age of eight. Prospective parents know as well. It can get dark inside the system, very dark indeed.

Now might be a good time to give a broad overview of how kids come into foster care in the first place, for those who don't have experience with the phenomenon. From a group of social workers who'd agreed to a collective interview, I asked for an outline, starting with home removal and ending in adoption, "to make it easier for people reading this book to understand."

They were strewn across couches and folding chairs in the children's recreation room of their facility. As if on cue, the social workers took strategic bites of pizza. Mouths too full to respond, they glanced at one another with bemused smiles.

Only one responded. "Your readers want a step-by-step guide for that process? Oooh, me too. That'd come in handy." A couple of them giggled.

Another added, "I do this for a living, and I've not seen an adoption happen twice the same way." Around the room, heads began to nod.

Keeping that caveat in mind, we can describe a few common patterns. Here's what the group came up with:

Social workers get involved when a teacher, neighbor, or other adult calls and reports something wrong in the home. The most common complaints include: there's no running water or food in the home; the kids are neglected, showing up to school hungry, dirty, inadequately clothed; it appears that somebody is hitting or otherwise hurting them, and the child has told an adult or the adult has observed repeated injuries.

Following up on these complaints, Child Protective Services (CPS) visits the house. If a worker for this division of DSS sees evidence of something wrong—injuries, overt fear beyond shyness, severe hygienic neglect, to name a few—they can choose between putting a safety plan in place or removing the child.

Elizabeth ("call me Liz") is a Family Preservation Services worker. She explains, "CPS prefers not to take a child without warning. We want first of all to leave the child in the home if that's realistic, not just that day but always. To do that we create a family management plan. This involves the family in making decisions about how best to keep the children safe in the home while correcting problems that may take longer to resolve. That is our first goal."

Failing that, the social worker on the scene will ask the mom or dad if there's a relative who could come take the children to their house and look after them until things at home can be cleared up or fixed. In rural parts of Coalton, it is common for extended-family members to live near one another, so Mamaw or Sis may show up within minutes. The children go home with them so long as the answers to a few simple safety questions are satisfactory, and if required they promise that the person who has caused the removal doesn't go near the kids.

Only at times of crisis does a family specialist (the job title varies) take a child out of his or her home or extended family immediately. Even if it looks as if removal may come later, the safety plan serves as a holding pattern, and the social worker may still try to pull people together for a family-management-plan meeting, asking various extended-family members to hold one another accountable for behaviors or attend counseling on anger management or other topics. Meanwhile, parents fearful of losing their children sometimes disappear between CPS visits.

If a child must be moved and a relative is not available, the ultimate goal is to find a place that will be more stable than the one the child is leaving. The CPS worker will call her supervisor, who will authorize the removal and an emergency placement or a short/long-term foster, as appropriate. The office has lists of prospective homes on file. Ideally, there will be time to do a little matching. In reality, most social workers carry a handful of names and phone numbers in their heads, of people whose homes the social workers know have spaces, or of families looking to adopt who will take in kids on short notice and have worked hard to ensure one of those memorized numbers is theirs.

Not to put too fine a point on it, CPS people don't want to drive back to an office with children terrified into hysterics kicking the backs of the car seats, puking and pooping in distress, if they will have no place to take them from there. The CPS worker hopes to limit the children's sense of unrest. It's not easy to be the person trying to reassure distraught young'uns when they see you as the person who just yanked the rug out from under their lives. That's not a pleasant situation for anyone.

There are exceptions, Liz adds. She has removed kids who were "so used to it, they sat waiting for me with their siblings lined up alongside them, each one of them clutching their favorite toy. They knew what was coming. Some have clung to my neck as I carried them out, saying, 'Thank you, thank you.' One child handed me a piece of paper, cool as a cucumber, and said, 'I'm supposed to tell you to call Mee-maw.'"

Nine of Liz's home visits to date have resulted in removals, and she can remember every single one of them. "You do not forget."

A CPS worker will remove a child immediately if there seems to be imminent danger, including hunger, severe illness, threat of flight, or visible signs of abuse. Workers don't often have police backup but could call for it, depending on the reputation of the family, whether there have been prior complaints and visits, and how the family reacted to those—assuming any of that information is known. Not all visits are prebriefed. Notes are not always available at the time a call is made.

Until recently, most Coalton removals happened because a teacher called from school. Social workers estimated anecdotally that until recent years this used to describe perhaps 90 percent of all investigations, but that's all changed now.

"Now, with the drug culture and that so-called war on drugs ongoing here, CPS workers are riding along in the patrol cars on midnight raids. Which means we remove kids in the middle of the night with all the trauma of arrests and search-and-seizure going on around them, sirens blaring, guns drawn, parents screaming and getting handcuffed. Then those kids are going to the ER to get checked out about half the time, and then back to somebody's office and crying themselves to sleep on a couch with a coat thrown over them, and we're sitting there beside them until daylight when we can start calling people."

The calls begin with colleagues in DSS, social workers specializing in family placement, foster-care specialists, adoption coordinators—again, the titles vary but the job remains the same: find a place the kids can go that matches the foster parents' preferences with a child's needs. A DSS questionnaire listing preferences like gender, age, personality, and physical traits is supposed to help in this effort. Parents fill it out when they go through the licensing procedure for fostering.

Liz laughs; there is no mirth in the sound. "Sounds great, right? Tell me what genius thinks after I've spent ten minutes with these traumatized children, I can look through the thirty-two of these [questionnaires] we have on file and find the ones that match. This child is sitting next to me, crying. 'Do you like dogs, honey? Look up so I can see what color your eyes are.'" Liz waves a hand in frustration, then seems to catch herself. "Of course, odds are strong we know these kids already, so it's not that bad. Plus, we take them to the ER to get checked out so we get more info right away."

Still, CPS workers try to avoid crisis placements. If they suspect that one might be coming, they keep a list of potential matches in mind, reviewing available homes for preferences or even calling foster parents they know to have a casual chat about "what might or might not happen."

"Then you pray for their availability the day it happens," Liz shrugs.

The availability of thirty-two licensed homes doesn't sound too bad in a county that last year had just under a hundred foster kids needing placement, does it? Yet the social workers say they use about ten of them, returning to those over and over. There are many reasons why, but a big one is the number of people who check "single child under six" on their preference forms.

"I can place them via phone, driving down the mountain," Liz says of children at that young age. "But what do you do with the six-, eight-, and thirteen-year-old siblings, and that oldest one cussing you up one side and down the other? How many homes have room for three at once, plus take kids in the teen years?"

Enter option number two. If DSS is willing to pay a supplemental fee, no fewer than seven private agencies in a three-county area of rural Coalton are contracted to work with the state to place children in therapeutic care; in urban areas, that number climbs. Many of these agencies deal with regular placements as well, which still cost the state more because they involve a fee for the agency to have trained and prepared the parents. DSS policy is to start with its own office's lists to find parents available for regular care, but often the social workers wind up calling private agencies.

There's no real rhyme or reason to how those calls go out. The DSS social worker puts the fishhooks in the water, describing the children as best she can to her counterpart at the agency. The private agency's social worker looks over his list of available homes and starts making phone calls. The first one to call back gets the kids.

"It's just about what you could imagine," says Cody, a director of one of those private agencies. "A friend at DSS called me last week at midnight; had three-year-old twin boys in her backseat . . ." Cody launches into a story.

The boys had been chewing on wood in their home because they were suffering from pica—a nutritional deficiency that causes people to eat non-food items—and acute malnutrition. That "behavioral problem" made the twins eligible for placement via therapeutic foster care. Cody placed them within the hour, and a day later he got a call from another friend at a different agency.

"He says to me, 'We wanted them! We've had parents waiting a long time!'"

Around the room, social workers roll their eyes, look away, shake their heads, throw loaded facial expressions Cody's way; one gives a snort that might be interpreted as *The only reason you're getting away with telling that story is you're the supervisor.*

Cody notices. "Yeah, it's a little unseemly how that part goes. Because that sibling group of three and the oldest one's a teenager? Yeah. They're gonna get split up." Workers nod, sigh, and refill their soda glasses.

From here, the process can turn murky. If the parents follow the family management plan put in place to help things at home—running water is installed, Uncle Bobby's put on a restraining order, Stepdad goes back to counseling, and the therapist cites progress—the kids might be returned. If Mom goes into drug treatment and the extended family have custody, the kids will go back after Mom gets out. If the state has the kids during that time, Mom is supposed to pass a drug test and appear in court. When all goes according to protocol, should she lose her sobriety later, the kids will be taken again for temporary placement until she gets clean. This is often how bouncing through the system begins for the kids.

Things happen in the order they're supposed to, or they don't. People do their jobs, or they don't. Parents get clean and stay that way, or they don't. Children go to a foster home, back to Mom, to a foster home, and back to Mom in stretches lasting three months to a year, depending on the family court's availability, Mom's progress, and the attention of the guardian ad litems and caseworkers to the nonstop flow of documents across their desk. (A guardian ad litem is someone appointed by the court to represent the legal interests of the children; sometimes they are therapists or other professionals, and sometimes Child Appointed Special Advocates, or CASA volunteers.)

There's nothing to stop the ebb and flow of returns and removals except a somewhat fluid set of court expectations or the advocacy of the ad litems. In the states within the Coalton area, a third party's being prepared to step in as parent can facilitate the termination of parental rights (voluntary or involuntary). Judges by far prefer seeing proof that adoption is imminent to making a child a ward of the state for any lengthy period.

The involuntary termination of parental rights requires proof that a parent has abused or neglected his or her child(ren) sufficiently to endanger the child's life and health, and that "reasonable efforts" to resolve these parental problems have failed. Each court visit tends to have deadlines attached to it, and the United States has a twenty-four-month deadline for enacting termination—but when the clock starts on that deadline can vary by judge. One of the stories in this book involves an involuntary termination that occurred within two months. Another took six years.

Dale, who was not at the "pizza meeting," later pointed out one reason for such variations. "Drug addicts lose their ability to provide a safe home for their children, not their wish to provide it. They'll fight. They'll try to get clean. They'll either make it, or they'll relapse. Which means the whole thing starts again."

It's a hard dance to watch under any circumstances, but when the clock is ticking toward the point when adoption is allowed, the waiting is the worst part for the child in question, her family, and her caseworkers.

"Once they realize Mom or Dad is never going to get it together, these kids long to be adopted. They want stability. And they know the older they get, the less likely adoption's going to take place. Once they hit double digits, their chances are melting away, and they're very aware of this, so they put on this hard veneer, act out trying to push people away, but you can see it. They're desperate to belong in a family before it's too late." Cody shakes his head in frustration.

Cami agrees. She's an eighteen-year-old college student who hit the foster care system at the age of four. She came to my bookstore to talk about the journey she and her younger sister, Debbie, began when Deb's biological father overdosed in front of them.

The girls, their mother, Bonnie, and Deb's dad, Al, lived in Troutdale, a town of one thousand residents that can really only be described as "dying." Their small cinderblock apartment sat in the middle of a row of three jutting over a flowing mountain stream, with upmarket fishing cabins dotting the hill on the other side. Troutdale hoped to save itself with sport tourism, but the cabins are owned mostly by local lawyers or bank managers.

Bonnie and her husband were frequent drug users. One day, Al fell without warning onto the kitchen floor. Cami's mother dropped to her knees and shook him, shouting, "Wake up. Al, wake up!"

Likely, these shouts-turned-to-screams alerted neighbors to phone the police; Cami doesn't remember anyone in their apartment making the call that brought sirens. Two or three ambulance people rushed into the room, while a large policeman grabbed Deb and Cami, one under each arm, hauling them outside.

Did that frighten her, you wonder?

"No, I was used to policemen coming to our apartment. They'd always been nice to us, just yelled at Mom and Dad a bit. What scared me was, I looked over his shoulder and saw them giving Al mouth-to-mouth resuscitation. I don't think I knew what it was then, but it scared me. I could tell it was something awful. Final."

The girls rode in the ambulance beside comatose Al and their sobbing mother. The mask on Al's face in the ambulance (one assumes it was for oxygen) had impressed both girls, so while they sat in the waiting room, they tried to make one from magazine pages.

Without warning, the police stormed in, heading straight for Bonnie with an unequivocal (and loud) message: she wasn't fit to be a mother; they were taking her children; she deserved to lose them. Bonnie cried, the hospital staff stared, and the police yelled. Cami and Deb forgot their paper masks and sat down, making no noise or movement. Experience had taught them that when adults were screaming, invisibility worked best.

But the instant the cops turned toward the girls, Deb went from wide-eyed silence to the kind of shriek only a toddler can produce. She ran from the officer, toward her family. (Cami is certain that no social worker was there, and she doesn't know why; that's not how these things are meant to go, according to social workers.) The police reassured both girls that it was okay, that they were taking them to a safe place. The officer tried to hold Debbie safely yet securely as he carried her out of the hospital, but the three-year-old, sensing rather than understanding that the world as she knew it had tilted into chaos, slid into a full-fledged flailing, kicking, terror-fueled meltdown.

"They had bruises. I guarantee it." Cami pauses, sitting on the green couch in the bookstore's classics room, and stares at the titles on the shelf across from her. She is a quiet, think-before-speaking girl, her brown hair cut in a no-nonsense bowl. Working summers as a lifeguard has left her skin almost as brown as her hair. "I think people watching would have described it as dramatic. I remember being embarrassed because everybody was staring at us."

It wasn't until another officer picked her up and headed toward the door that Cami realized—with a child's swift and certain clarity—what Deb had already grasped.

This time was different.

"And I think Bonnie did too, because she started crying even more and acting crazy like I'd never seen before, and then I don't remember anything until we pulled into a parking lot and an old lady met us and said we should get in her car."

Within a day or so, Cami and Deb had figured out that they were in some kind of temporary shelter, going back to their mother's "soon, but not today," and that the little old lady was "kinda nuts but in a sweet way." The rules were simple: be good, and on Saturday you got a new toy. Other kids came and went; the sisters stayed.

Time flows differently when you're four; Cami doesn't know how many months they were there, just that she started school and joined Deb in calling the lady "Mom"—which really upset Bonnie when she phoned. Cami and Debbie didn't know that she was trying to get clean and get her daughters back; when their weekly news report included, "Mom made us brownies," Bonnie shouted back down the line, "She's not your mom!"

Sometime in the spring, the girls went back to Bonnie's apartment over-looking the stream. That became the pattern; she sobered up and got a job; they returned; she'd get high or in trouble with the law; and they'd be taken away from her and go to a foster home until she got them back again.

A kid doesn't necessarily notice patterns. Each move is just what's happening then. Cami thinks it might have been six placements over the course of three years, but by the time she was seven, it had dawned on her that she and her sister would never live at home for any length of time again. Looking back on those bounces, Cami wonders, "Why didn't all those judges giving her custody have a lick of common sense between them?"

Cami describes with something between disgust and sorrow how her mother once went to the courthouse bathroom, took a pill, passed out, and hit her head on the sink. A few minutes later, Bonnie walked into family court with a paper towel stuck to her bleeding head, said she had slipped on wet tile in the bathroom, and swore she was drug-free and able to look after "my girls that I love more than life."

Cami doesn't know why a drug test wasn't involved. Protocol dictated it should have been. Hearing the story later, Cody suggests a couple of possibilities. "I wasn't there, I don't know, but it could have been the ad litem was sick, or late. The judge was in a hurry. They're not into returning kids to drugged-up parents, so something sure went wrong. It happens. It's not supposed to, but supposing it does, how's a little kid gonna tell the judge, 'Excuse me, Your Honor, you're supposed to check her hair and her pee'?"

Reflecting on that moment, Cami has one wish. "As an adult now I want to go back and ask the judge what was on his mind that day. Lunch?"

Bonnie was trying to get it together. But as any who have suffered it personally or by proxy know, the illness of addiction overpowers instinct and reason alike. It also cripples love, but who wants to admit that? Addicted people tend to be incapable of looking after anybody, themselves included, so court-ordered removals are less about who loves whom than about a child's safety. Lots of people loved Debbie and Cami, including their bio mom and extended-family members on both sides, but the task of providing them with a safe, warm place to grow up would fall to a succession of foster homes—some up to the job, some not.

Cami and Deb had maternal family in the region who declined to take custody, and the only comment Cami offers on this was that she and her sister would have liked to have avoided a few of the homes that fostered them. She does not talk about most of her foster homes. It is embarrassing to be a victim.

"Any way you slice it, by the time a child enters foster care, they've been rejected more than some adults are their whole lives," Cody told me once. "They should all be in therapeutic care. What they've had to endure wouldn't leave some grown-ups standing."

He could have been describing Cami and Deb. Stability for the sisters was out of the question in the bouncy castle of foster care that followed. Sometimes safety was too. Working hard to create their own security as much as possible, they tried to play by the rules—whenever they could figure them out.

"We tried to be good," Cami says, straight-cut bangs flopping into her dark eyes as she shakes her head and shrugs. Each place had a different set of rules; what was fine, even expected in one place might be forbidden in the next. Things like using the stove unsupervised, choosing which television shows to watch, being expected to complete chores that you hadn't done before and thus didn't know how to handle.

In one home that meant vacuuming. Cami had never used a vacuum before.

"She had to explain it to me. And she kept saying how awful it was that I didn't know, kind of overly sweet, 'It's not your fault, dear.'" Cami's jaw tightens.

Some foster homes said clearly what was expected; in others, the girls had to figure it out. At first, Cami and Deb tried to be good because they wanted to go back home to Mom. Then they were good because they realized that Mom was never going to get it together, so they needed to get adopted. Good kids get adopted first.

More precisely, Cami thought that they needed to get adopted. Deb lost interest. If this was going to be life from now on, then . . .

Cami's eyes roll toward the ceiling, and her face lightens with a bemused smile. "I love my sister. I loved her then; I love her now. Oh, but she could be a real devil."

One of their foster homes included the family's bio daughter, a blond like Debbie of just about the same age. The two took an instant dislike to each other, probably fueled by Deb's overt envy of her anti-twin. One day,

Deb took the scissors from the drawer only adults were allowed to open and barbered the heads of every doll the bio daughter had.

Straight to the car, I bet, Cami thought when she saw what her sister had done. Sure enough, the caseworker showed up, but only to give everyone a talking to about safety. The sisters didn't leave for another three months, when Bonnie had enough of a clean streak going to petition for return.

Stories about the tensions and alliances between birth and foster children could fill an entire book. Comedy and tragedy rage in these situations. At another home, Deb broke a house rule and got mad at the foster mother over losing TV privileges. She sneaked into the dining room, took the china plates that were Foster Mom's pride and joy from their special cabinet, and smashed them in a big pile on the dining room floor. Cami took one look, went to their room, and packed garbage bags for both of them. Sure enough, Foster Mom called their social worker, in tears.

In the car, as the caseworker drove away from that former placement in grim silence, Cami turned and pummeled her little sister. "You jerk! I liked them!" Deb grinned and retaliated. The girls slapped and punched until the social worker threatened to pull the car over.

"Now that I know social workers have to do case notes on the time they spend with foster kids, I wonder what that poor woman wrote that night," Cami says, grimacing.

That's the way it went for a while, with Deb pulling the strings and Cami playing the good girl. Despite Deb's antics, usually the sisters didn't get kicked out of homes; they just went from foster parents to Bio Mom and back to fosters as Bonnie got clean, blew it, and tried again. Ironically, the other time Cami remembers when a difficult behavior precipitated their removal, the blame fell on her.

"I love animals, all animals. The family had this puppy, and it was so cute, but I was maybe eight or nine, and I didn't see it and I backed up and stood on the puppy's leg and broke it. Then the woman called and had us taken out of the home. They wouldn't believe I hadn't done it on purpose. I still swear to you—it's like ten years later we're talking about this, and I still swear—I didn't mean to. I would never have done that on purpose. I love animals. I just didn't see the puppy. But we were out."

That particular foster home had been looking for an excuse to send them away, the girls knew. Unable to have children of their own, the couple wanted to adopt. Cami and Debbie weren't yet available for adoption; besides, these foster parents wanted just one child, and younger. Although sometimes it's just a personality mismatch—you are not the child these foster parents are looking for—in other cases those seeking to adopt get frustrated that the kids in their house are not available because someone is trying to regain custody.

Eventually, an unspoken message wafts through the home: hurry up and leave so we can find our forever kid. It's not unusual for kids to pick up on such clues in the vibe of a house. In fact, foster children who lack the skill to discern what kind of place they're in might have a rough row to hoe. Cami swears she got so good at it, she could tell on the car ride to their new location whether these were people fostering with the intent to adopt, for a paycheck, out of kindness, or for some other reason.

A parent who drives in silence may not be emotionally invested. The silent ones might be interested strictly in the minimum they would be required to provide without getting their license pulled—in which case, start hiding food in your room right away. Or they could be more the "don't bother me and here are the rules and there's the fridge, now let's just get along" types. Others might say differently, Cami added with her characteristic caution, but in her experience the silent drivers rarely turned into forever family.

By contrast, an adult who asks several questions, wanting to know too much, too fast, could be either an overeager adopter (and, therefore, a potential sitting duck when it comes to discipline) or a manipulative and dangerous foster parent looking for your vulnerabilities. Foster kids learn to be careful about divulging information that could make them targets for specific punishments or mental cruelty. In the same way that Deb went after the foster mother's plates, knowing how much the woman loved them, foster parents with control issues tend to look for what hurts an individual child the most.

Sometimes the rides were just downright surreal, as with the lady who picked the sisters up for respite care while their foster family took a break. They were going to stay with her for a month only, and everybody knew it, so no one had anything to hide or protect. That may or may not shed some light on the woman's first question to Cami.

"She got us in the car and she looks at me—Deb was in the backseat—and she said, 'Do you know the difference between a frog and a toad?' I'm staring at her, and I kind of shake my head, 'No, I don't.' So then she explained it all while we're driving, legs and tails and stuff."

Cami did not retain much of the lecture on amphibian anatomy, but her memories of that house were "friendly craziness." About twenty minutes after they'd been shown around and left to unpack their black garbage sacks, the respite mom came to tell them her family was coming over for a welcome party. The girls had been there less than an hour before the grill was fired up, the family setting out tubs of potato salad, a big ol' backyard barbecue going down in all its glory.

"We were kinda weirded out at first, but then they gave us sparklers."

The girls' next foster placement was via KinCare; the grandmother of Deb's father had gotten into a position to ask for custody. They stayed more than a year and, although still in elementary grades, thought they might actually graduate high school under Gammy's care. But one day they came home from school, and there sat Bonnie on the porch swing, waving a court order.

Bonnie had brought along her latest boyfriend to help with the driving because she planned to move the girls to another state. They threw toys, clothes, and bikes into the station wagon and headed out. The ride turned long and unpleasant. Helpless with fury, the sisters kicked the seat backs, screaming and crying, "Take us back, take us back to Gammy!"

After a few rounds of demands to return versus commands to quit crying, Bonnie looked in the rearview mirror and locked eyes with Cami. "If you don't stop, for every minute you scream I'm going to throw a toy out the window," she said.

Debbie shrieked again. Bonnie reached over the seat and threw a toy out.

"She was younger. She had more toys. I quit for her sake, and she quit after three or four more toys went flying."

Four months went by before Bonnie passed out again. Cami picked up the phone, dialed 911, and asked for the paramedics and Child Protective Services. When stability devolves to chaos, as a long-term foster child assumes it inevitably will, you hold your breath and wait for the adult in charge to do something wrong so you can get out of there. Then you go back to following the rules in the homes that look after you between returns until . . .

Until something, and while no one can really say what that turning point will be, for most bouncing kids, it's either aging out (turning eighteen in

foster care) or court termination of parental rights because someone wants
to adopt you. Cami remembers very well the first day of her final placement, when the Match was made. After she and Deb unpacked their sacks,
they headed back toward the living room. Overhearing the woman of the
house on the phone, they paused out of sight to listen.

"Most foster kids are great eavesdroppers. Don't judge us. It's a survival skill."

On this occasion, she heard the woman tell her husband, "The new kids
have arrived. I know we asked for a boy, but the youngest girl just turned
nine last week, and she has an older sister. They're devoted to each other
so social services didn't want to split them up."

Hmm, that's how they sold us, Cami thought, *because Debbie is sorta the
right age.*

Despite this rocky beginning, that home became permanent for Cami.
It was also here that she learned to cook with some modicum of safety.

During the yo-yo times when the girls were returned to Bonnie, it fell
to Cami as the oldest to concoct some sort of supper and weekend meals.
Since the age of three, she'd been able to microwave, and during returns in
the early bouncing years she had learned to boil water—a skill that scared
some of her foster parents when she demonstrated mastery over lighting
a gas stove. Recognizing how easy it would be to burn herself or set the
house afire, Cami pretty much confined her bio-home culinary adventur-
ing to pizza rolls, cereal, and sandwiches. If it couldn't be zapped or eaten
from the box, she didn't try it.

Some foster kids get pretty good at a recipe called Ramen Ugh: scour the
car floor, steal, or beg for enough change to buy a block of cream cheese
and a packet of ramen noodles. Let the cream cheese get soft in a bowl, and
with your hands knead in the spices and noodles. Wait until the noodles get
a little soft, and pass out spoons. One cream cheese and three ramen pack-
ets will fill up five smallish kids. The name and exact recipe for this break-
fast/dinner/supper of champions enjoys regional variations, and there are
other simple "meals" of equally ingenious dubiety. A foster child's recipe
collection is fascinating, if not appetizing.

If Bonnie forgot to bring easy-prep foods into the house before a bender,
the girls didn't eat; free breakfast at school the next morning would make
up for it. Weekends were the worst; Friday night to Monday morning is a

long stretch without food. Cami was eager to acquire cooking skills as a self-protective measure against the next return. The house that had wanted one boy eight or younger instead of two girls nine and eleven wound up being where she learned the basics.

However, Deb's adoption into the same home was contested by members of her father's family; Gammy was gone, but her father's sister wanted her. Recognizing that Deb was about to get firepower behind her adoption due to the zeal of an aunt who was pushing for involuntary termination of Bonnie's parental rights, a guardian ad litem stepped in to help Cami. As noted, ad litems are court-appointed legal representatives for the children. Don't confuse them with caseworkers; the job of the ad litem is solely to represent the best interests of the child during court proceedings. A child can have multiple ad litems over the course of his case, which is not ideal. Cami had several, none of them much help in her opinion, "until this one. She was with CASA."

CASA volunteers have a great reputation throughout the United States and are in constant demand. Often retirees, CASA men and women pass multiple background checks before they are allowed to work on any cases. Once assigned to a child, they interview the relevant parties and then present the judge with background information and a recommendation. According to the CASA trainers in Coalton's University City, judges rule in alignment with the ad litems' recommendations more than 90 percent of the time.[1]

Cami can't praise her CASA assistant enough. "She saw what had been happening and that I was about to lose my sister along with everything else. It's unusual for siblings never to be separated in foster care, but we never were until the adoptions."

When Deb's bio family asserted its claim, it didn't include Cami because she had a different father. Knowing how wrenching the separation would be on the girl who had been mother to her little sister for so long, Cami's ad litem asked the couple who taught her to cook if they wanted to adopt her. Then the ad litem used the years of bouncing and the loss of Deb as arguments for finally granting an involuntary termination of Bonnie's parental rights.

"Something somebody should have done years before," said the University City CASA supervisor with whom I reviewed Cami's adoption. "That's all I'm gonna say."

Hard though it was for the sisters to separate, Cami still thought it was "just about the best thing that could have happened to us." The sisters attended different schools and maintained close contact via phone and social media. After Cami graduated high school, she moved cross-country to be near Deb, and got married. She is now in her second year of college and plans to become a juvenile probation officer.

"And when I turn twenty-one, I'll be a CASA volunteer."

4

Two Reboot Camps

People get into fostering to heal themselves from their own childhood trauma. Which really means, they think they are healed from it, and they're ready to give back, save some kids from the hell they lived through. They get five kids in their home and then something happens with a kid that triggers them and you wind up focusing all your therapy on the parent rather than the kid.

If you come from chaos, you don't know halfway to normal isn't normal. Please don't foster unless you've got your shit together. Better yet, don't foster until somebody else tells you you've got your shit together. Because when the shit hits the fan, you're going to give up. Or worse. It's not a moral failing to spend your life getting your own shit together; you're not required to dive back into that pool of darkness to try and save somebody else. Don't believe the Lifetime TV movies. Just holding your own life together is triumph enough.

—family therapist

I remember them arriving like it was yesterday. This little four-year-old dropped off with the black bags, and she and her older brother explored outside awhile, then I called them in for dinner. They really didn't know they were in foster care. It was all brand new to them. Their mom was supposed to report to jail for drug trafficking, but she'd made no arrangements in the weeks leading up to it. That day the kids went to school like always, with no plans for who was going to pick them up that evening because she'd be in jail. She told DSS the teachers would take care of it, and that's how they came into foster care.

And the four-year-old sat at my table and she said, "Is y'all a foster family?" And I said yes. And she said, "Is y'all a nice foster family?" And I said, "Well, I think so, but I guess you'll have to decide if that's true or not."

—foster mom

IN PREVIOUS chapters, we've seen that foster families are often motivated by a desire to have children of their own. For a smaller group, altruism begets their entry into the world of foster care. Altruism in the Coalfields is many times indistinguishable from religious conviction. Outside Coalton, a list of do-gooders would include humanists, pagans, nontheists, Universalists, and so on. Within the region, multiple denominations of mountain Christianity fuel most of the fire.

Social workers narrow their eyes when foster parents see children as projects to make the world better, rather than as individuals. "It's a fine line between someone who says she wants to change a child's life, and someone out to change the world. You need to listen closely to how they ask questions. Watch how they go through the classes. Are they looking for a guaranteed soul to save, or are they ready to be true parents?" So says Dale, the forty-two-year-veteran social worker who also pastors a local church.

Doing good is sometimes motivated by an adult's hoping to give someone else's child a better life than she had. Some 60 percent of foster parents in Coalton were adopted or fostered children, say the social workers in the region.[1] Dale points out that the number may actually be higher because some adults were raised by grandparents but never formally adopted.

Most people agree that we tend to revert to how we were raised when raising our children. It is inevitable, unless we do a lot of soul-searching and maybe some therapy. Social workers describe foster parents (as well as themselves) as coming less from a broad swath of life experiences than from two opposing ends of a continuum, united by the common goal of giving other people's children a happy, safe launch into adulthood.

We all know that motivations for fostering or adopting must be as varied as humanity itself, but when social workers in Coalton talk for any length of time, the "we are looking for a human rainbow of experiences" recruiting speech dissolves into stories of mentoring two kinds of parents. In the first camp sit stable people who had a comfortable upbringing and want to spread the love; you met Abigail and John in chapter 1 and will meet Sam and Becky in chapter 5. The second camp consists of adults who had rough childhoods; often they were in foster care or adopted, or raised by relatives in a nebulous deal even less formal than Kim's as related in chapter 2. This second group tends to be perceived as wanting to redeem their own childhoods by making life better for others. They want to make a difference to someone, to pay attention in the way attention wasn't paid to them. Authorities differ on the effectiveness of those who truly fall into this camp. Psychologists and clinicians tend to suggest that "up from hell" individuals are in for such a rough ride that they might not be able to become part of the solution.

Licensed Clinical Social Worker (LCSW) Cassie is one of three therapists in the Walker City–University City–Troutdale–Great Rock square. She is succinct about foster parents who were foster kids.

"They come from chaos. They have lived in darkness. And unless they have done an awful lot of work, when the going gets tough, they revert to chaos and darkness." Cassie lifts her hands to the sky, palms up. "Which makes it hard for everyone." But they also make up more than half of Coalton's adopting and fostering parents, "so you get used to working with them." They need a lot of working with, she adds, raising her eyebrows.

On the other hand, social workers lament that the happy-upbringing team can get stuck in believing that, because they were "raised right," they should parent that way. When "that way" doesn't work with their foster kids, a lot of late-night phone calls to the caseworkers result. Social workers welcome all fosters, but they particularly like empty nesters because they are experienced parents. Yet they plan to do a lot of hand-holding with them as they become fosters because, ironically, those who have raised families are often the most "horrified" at the behavior of their new kids. The comments of social workers describing this dynamic could be boiled down into something along the lines of *They think we're soft because we treat the kids like victims instead of kids, and they've done this before, and what do we know with our twenty-four-year-old brains and our book learning?*

That's why there are licensing requirements for foster parents and even more intense classes for therapeutic foster parents: to teach the new skills these experienced parents will need to add to their arsenals. But not everyone sees their value in the heat of the moment. Nor does every foster parent walk into those required classes with eyes wide open; some, in the words of Sarcasm Master Cody, "hope to break the cycle of substance abuse, incarceration, and neglect without getting mud on their white shag carpets."

Most are not quite that naïve; Cody just likes a good sound bite. He also once said, "In one sense, they're exactly who we're looking for; they usually do it for kindness and from experience. But if they think they can parent the same way twice, God and righteousness on their side, and everything turn out for the best, we're gonna be in trouble. I'm not trying to put down their beliefs, but until they get their first foster kids, they don't know beans about this brave new world they're facing. The kids they're taking in have faced things in their lives these people never even had nightmares about, and they don't know it. That leads to at best a lot of sleepless nights, at worst heartache and broken promises. Don't forget, we're desperate for people who want to foster, so we're not turning anyone away unless they're rotten. But we know they're gonna have problems they don't anticipate. And we know these are the very people who don't want someone else to help them with their problems. They're self-possessed; they don't like to ask for help. It's like the thing that draws them to being good foster parents makes them bad at it too."

A casual observer like me begins to wonder: who's better at fostering, those who walked that lonesome valley of dysfunction in their own families, or the products of happy childhoods? Dale says that that's the wrong question to ask. "Do you have a teachable, compassionate, and patient personality? That's my question." If so, Dale says he doesn't care if you were raised by wolves or neurosurgeons, he wants to talk to you about foster parenting.

"If you're a compassionate person, genuinely wanting to invest in someone else, you're who we're looking for, because you're who our kids need."

Measured by Dale's yardstick, both camps of foster parents share the compassionate goal of redirecting a child's troubled history into a happy future, but they face different challenges in getting there. Or perhaps not.

Barbie, a fairly new social worker asked to comment on her observations of the differences between these two sets of parents, gives me an enigmatic look and suggests the distinctions are moot.

"People aren't beating our door down, to be honest, so we'll take either one if they know what they're getting into. But here's one thing: the doctors and lawyers and teachers in the nice safe homes that read the newspapers about foster kids getting into drugs and a life of crime, they think these kids are not fixable. They've seen the horror films about orphans and think our kids will murder you in your sleep. The parents who were fosters themselves know better."

She pauses, then adds, "Besides, I've met plenty of fucked-up lawyers and doctors I wouldn't trust with my dog. Having money doesn't make you a better parent."

Barbie has a way with words, although I hadn't been thinking of money so much as a pleasant childhood experience. But she has hit on how a stable upbringing tends to become a stable adulthood complete with a career, house, family, the works.

I turned to foster parents who had been foster children to seek their thoughts. Single mom Ronna has a way with girls. Ronna lives well outside Coalton now but grew up in the same area of Troutdale where Cami's bio mother, Bonnie, lived. A former foster child, Ronna takes in only girls; we talked by telephone because she had recently broken her foot.

Taken into the system at the age of four, she was adopted; but when she was fourteen, the adoption was disrupted (her adopting parents asked the court to take her back into state care), and she went to live in a group home until she turned eighteen. In her adoptive home, Ronna remembers "an enormous lack of emotional connection, no verbal communication and more importantly positive verbal communication. No 'Ronna, I love you,' but also no questions as simple as 'Are you hungry; what would you like to eat?' Stuff like that. Unless I was in trouble. Then there was all the talking, yelling, and hitting."

"Now my adoptive parents were not former fosters, but I do believe that they had their own agenda, and money played a huge roll in that. They received money for me but rarely used that money on me."

Ronna became a foster parent by offering respite care. Sometimes foster children aren't allowed to cross state lines; because of that, or family dynamics, or a host of other reasons, they stay home from weddings or funerals involving their foster parents' biological families. Respite parents also provide emergency overnights. And babysitting for established fosters: like all parents, sometimes couples want to get away for a weekend. Respite care is how many foster parents test the waters to see if they're interested in a greater commitment.

I asked Ronna what she thought about the "sunny side versus the dark valley" parental background. She heaved a sigh that reverberated down the phone line and offered her reasons for why former foster kids make excellent foster parents: they're familiar with the foibles of the system and don't waste time; they have highly polished skills for reading people's body language and voice inflections; and they understand more about the fears and hopes their charges bring with them than those who haven't been there.

"Even though we're talking about parents needing to be humble and flexible, which I agree with, I realized pretty early what motivated each of the girls, how we could make the most progress. That's important. Foster kids are good at reading people because we grew up having to do it. That's a useful skill when working with kids you never met before."

At the time we talked, Ronna was keeping sisters originally meant to stay a couple of months at most but who had been there a whole school year by the time their foster home decided not to have them return. That unspecified time frame touches on something Ronna feels passionate about. "It's so important not to have low expectations just because they're fosters. We foster kids don't want to just survive; we want to thrive."

Ronna resisted making the expected shortness of the girls' stay an excuse to be lax with them. "'Oh, I don't really have to invest since they'll be leaving any minute now.' That's an easy attitude to get, but it wouldn't have helped. Then, too, I didn't want to go all overdrive and stuff their little heads with everything you think a kid should know by age six the first week."

Ronna laughs. "In the classes, they said over and over that kids weren't used to having adults in charge, especially the oldest sibling, who would assume a watching role over the others. I was an only child [while adopted], but I remember acting out because I was trying to figure things out. They said over and over that kids need structure, and will fight against having it, but really benefit from it. That is so true.

"I remember the day they came. I turned them loose to explore the apartment and the little garden out back. The older sister came in and said something about picking flowers, and I said they weren't ours so we couldn't pick them, but we could walk around out there and enjoy them whenever we wanted. It was so cute. She balled her little fists up and hunched her shoulders and said, 'Ooooh, I *hate* it when the adults are in charge!'"

Ronna believes that it's less scary for children once they accept that an adult is going to look after them. "I think when we're young, we're afraid when we can do anything we want to do. When they feel they can't because 'Oh, that mean foster mother will not let me,' the pressure falls away from them. That behavior is off the table; they don't have to worry about it, even if they yell and kick at first."

I did ask Ronna one other question: why did she take only girls over the age of six, given that respite care is very broad-ranging in who needs it? She sighed again.

"Ok, this is going to make me sound lazy and stupid, but the first reason is, I never changed a diaper. In my whole life. I'm not ready to start to learn now, so it's kids old enough to not need them. As for girls . . ."

Ronna launches into a story from before her adoption. She spent time in two foster homes, and in one had an older foster brother. He accused the family of abusing him; the home was investigated, and during the investigation, as is required, the foster kids were moved. Ronna doesn't comment on whether she believes the boy was abused;[2] instead, she describes the experience. "I got out of school one day, and there's my caseworker, and she says, 'I've got your stuff, get in,' and that's how I knew he'd accused them of something. They don't tell us anything, but we know anyway."

Coupled with that experience, her wider inside knowledge of the system overall, and the classes she took, Ronna feels that girls are less likely to make false accusations against other women.[3] "I'm not saying it can't happen, just that it feels safer to me. Plus, there are a lot more girls out there that need help than boys, and I want them to be safe. I know they'll be safe with me. So."

Cody affirms Ronna's observation; about 85 percent of the cases his workers have are girls. He also picks up on Ronna's gap in life experiences. "Who would've taught her [to change a diaper]? Only children don't learn to change diapers either, but it freaks people out, what these kids do and don't know. They can't believe some of the things they've never done, and some of the things they have. It's all out of whack with America."

As to false accusations, Cody heaves a sigh reminiscent of Ronna's (whom he has never met). "They happen. We investigate. Procedures roll in and take over. We lose good people that way. And we weed out bad."

The power balance during accusations against adults can make who's in charge a bit tricky, Beth agreed at one of our bakery lunches. But it's not just a careful relationship-building between kids and parents that's happening. Social workers are sometimes accused of trying to undermine discipline with "soft victim-mentality syndrome—or something like that. It's not an official name. They just think we're making too many excuses."

Beth launches into a story about one particularly dark and stormy night. In the midst of any and all chaotic moments—be it a court's return of the child to the bio parents, behavioral issues in the home, school paperwork, or something else—social workers want foster parents to believe that they are on the parents' side. Even when giving advice the family doesn't want to hear. Social workers with active cases are required to carry phones with them at all times and not to leave the county when they're on emergency-call duty.

Beth's phone rang at about 11:00 p.m.; it was a foster father in Great Rock worried about the little girl who'd been in their home for two weeks. A petite blond reminiscent of a china doll, Amy was not given to tantrums. Considered quiet, intelligent, and articulate, she'd been having "a complete meltdown" for a couple of hours; the distraught dad described the little girl as throwing herself on the ground like a rag doll, leaping into their garbage cans, vomiting as she ran from them, screaming. The trigger, said her foster dad, had been a hamburger.

"First clue," says Beth, leaning forward and going into what can only be described as an all-systems-alert social worker's posture. Her shoulders tense, her eyebrows knit together, and she flicks black hair off her shoulder with a dismissive gesture before tapping the table with one long finger. "Nobody has a three-hour tantrum over food. Something else is going on; just got to help them figure out what."

The family had eaten home-cooked burgers at around 5:30 for the evening meal. Amy wasn't hungry. No problem, her parents said; they'd reheat her meal when she was ready to eat; run along and play, dear. By 8:00 p.m., Amy was hungry, but a thunderstorm had knocked out power in the neighborhood. Her foster father offered peanut butter and jelly or a bowl of cereal, whichever she wanted. Amy said she wanted the burger. Dad explained they had no way to heat the patty back to a safe temperature, and because bacteria grew in meat, which he knew Amy was smart enough to understand, that option was, so to speak, off the table. However, maybe he could rustle up some cheese and crackers if she'd rather?

Nine-year-old Amy went into overdrive on the tantrum from hell. They tried to ride it out, but by the time they rang Beth, the parents were exhausted and nearly inarticulate with what she categorized as "maybe fear, maybe embarrassment." The couple were in the process of trying to adopt Amy, but Beth could hear all their plans unraveling as the child pitched this demon fit.

"I had to try and talk these very educated, very nice upper-middle-class parents down from the ledge. It's like you do all this foster training with them before they start, and you cover things like this, but then when it happens, their mind goes black. The house is full of rage and confusion, plus they're dealing with their own expectations. A kid in your home, your cozy nest where you make the rules but you don't know them yet as a person, and she loses her mind? You're not prepared for this kind of—well, they were calling it violence. Plus, from my point of view as a social worker, the unknown includes the unspoken history that these events will bring up from the parents' own childhoods."

The parents went back and forth on the phone, one keeping up with Amy, the other talking to Beth. The social worker elicited the information that the couple had told Amy about the pending adoption—her first inkling that she wasn't going home.

Bingo, Beth thought, as the clock ticked toward midnight. But how to get across to the family this thing that Beth could now see had happened?

Shortly after, the mother said into the receiver, "I didn't let my previous children indulge in such temper tantrums. Amy cannot expect to continue to behave this way in my home. She has to learn she can't manipulate us."

Beth felt a glimmer of hope. *OK, that's progress. They recognize it's about control.* She suggested the parents reframe Amy's desperation less as pitting her will against theirs than as trying to control at least one element of her life. Amy had only recently been moved from an emergency foster home to this one and hadn't known until her new parents-to-be told her that her mother's rights had been involuntarily terminated. Very quickly.

While that swift move may have seemed positive to everyone else, Amy wasn't excited about being up for adoption. She didn't need rescuing, thank you very much; she had everything arranged just as she liked it in her birth home. An only child of gifted intelligence, she ran the show there while acing everything at school. Controlling an addicted mom was a mere piece of her daily routine to be managed, like paying the household bills and shopping for groceries—which she also did.

"You can see how delicate this was for me, trying to put that nicely in the midst of the craziness, and you can see why the parents couldn't grasp the information," Beth says, shoulders heaving in a sigh. "Who wants to hear that the child you're trying to save doesn't want you?"

Amy's case slid through the system in a way other kids could only dream about, with parental rights terminated almost immediately, and then the first foster family after emergency care wanting to adopt her. It is an outcome some kids bouncing through the system would have given their right arm for, but Amy hadn't yet adjusted to resigning as executive director of her own life.

Beth rolls her shoulders in frustration. "I felt like screaming at these people, 'Burger, schmurger!' Getting adopted instead of going home: *that's* what her three-hour full-body meltdown is about. You want to call a nine-year-old who got herself dressed and ready for school, pulled in straight As, and managed the home's finances a brat because she's freaked at losing all that responsibility? Did you think she'd be grateful for a chance to love you?"

Permit me to interrupt Beth's telling of the Phone Call from Hell to interject a comment that therapist Cassie offered at one of our talks: if there's an overarching emotion she sees governing childhood for foster kids, it is the frustration of feeling out of control. Adults around them—some who care, some who don't, some whom the kids have never met—make decisions that affect their lives, and they have nothing to say about it. Sometimes they don't know the decision is being made, as was the case with Amy. And they're in the system in the first place because they've been betrayed by adults who were supposed to care about them more than anyone else.

"Small wonder they pitch fits. As an adult, in situations of frustration or betrayal, I've had my share of meltdowns. But a foster kid's supposed to maintain equilibrium, or he's labeled." Cassie shrugs.

Back to Amy's story. The couple seeking to adopt her had, in Beth's opinion, psychoanalyzed themselves into a corner. They believed the problem was food insecurity. They kept saying things like, "We offered her a PBJ. She knows we're not trying to starve her; we won't let her be hungry." When Beth brought up control, they batted it aside. "She's got to learn she's not in charge."

But she has been, and she knows she's about to lose that. Beth tried again. "'Fine, but you don't seem to realize that she didn't get asked where she wanted to live. Now she has a completely new family structure, and she's enraged because she feels helpless. She needs to feel she has some control over something.' And these educated people, they come back to me saying, 'Are you telling us to just go get her a burger?' and I'm so frustrated I feel like shouting—which you do not do on those phone calls; you keep your voice even and calm. 'No, I'm saying stop seeing this as insanity and see it as a natural consequence of the life changes she's had in the last two weeks. Tell her she's not in this alone, that you're listening to her even when she's screaming the information at you. Tell her she should never have had to be the person in charge, but that changing that isn't going to be as bad as she thinks it will.'"

The parents didn't accept Beth's advice. "I think they saw talking to her about control as rewarding bad behavior. They wanted to nip tantrums in the bud, to let her know she couldn't have them in their home. I hear it all the time from first-time foster parents: they will make positive impacts on these children's lives. A week later they're on the phone, yelling, 'All your advice is psychobabble mumbo jumbo; kids can't be allowed to make the rules; they've never been told no, never had any structure in their homes; we're going to impose order, discipline'—all that crap."

Beth rests her head briefly on the table in front of her, then comes up as if for air. "If I had a dollar for every time I held a conversation like that, I could buy my own Caribbean island. In five years of working cases, I've had exactly one child who was truly psychopathic and out of control. The rest just had tantrums. Show me a kid who hasn't thrown a tantrum in his life." Her sudden laugh holds a tinge of bitterness. "For that matter, show me a foster kid who doesn't have good reason to throw one."

Yet some foster parents do break through and succeed, even under the most provoking circumstances. As Ronna pointed out, one skill foster children are pretty good at can prove unfortunate when used against parents. Most kids raised in the system become adept at reading people; that means they excel at picking out what matters most to a foster parent and using it against them when the going gets tough.

Vulnerability is not always a good thing in human relationships, at least not at first as foster child and foster parent get to know each other. Beth tells another story, shaking her head. Maurice was about nine when he went to live with Eve in a two-bedroom house in Walker City. Eve started proceedings to adopt him when he turned ten. Holding down a part-time job, Eve received therapeutic-care funding for Maurice. Soon after he arrived, Eve began to fix up her aluminum-sided bungalow.

"Eve got new floors, hardwood. We tell parents to lock up their knives and scissors, all their dangerous stuff. Maurice knew those floors were the most important things in the house; Eve took him along to help pick them out; they were all she talked about. She mentioned the floor to me no less than three times when I saw her for an appointment about Maurice's grades."

Of course, when he got mad at her for refusing to allow him to join a ball team, Maurice took a butter knife to her brand-new hardwood floors. Foster parenting classes cover locking away where the kids can't reach them those things that are important or dangerous, but floors really can't be protected in that way.

"These kids have had things taken away from them in ten moves already," Beth says with a sigh. "The fact that they're not feeling respect for your grandmother's quilt is natural fallout from the way they've lived so long, not an early-warning sign of how their whole life with you might be. Take it easy and avoid tragic mistakes."

In the aftermath of the butter-knife scarring, Eve asked her son-in-training if he felt the floor was more important to her than he was. Maurice refused to discuss this, sitting in stony silence, so Eve let him know that (1) the floors were not more important than Maurice's well-being, (2) nothing he could do would make Eve stop taking care of him, and (3) his allowance was halved until the damage had been paid for. Maurice is still in Eve's home, has been adopted, and is about to graduate from high school. Eve added other home improvements during his stay, including a porch and an above-ground pool.

5

Doing Good, Well

We really do have a good bunch of people in our school system, but the first year my husband and I did this, it was touch and go. Fostering's like the Clash of the Titans—two systems, both claiming the law on their side, neither one interested in the needs of the child so long as they can keep their own butts covered.

We got our first foster daughter halfway through the school year, and she got put into a class for special-needs kids that was all boys. Ninety percent of the boys in there were foster kids, and our daughter had some social issues. So I went to the school and said, "This is just asking for trouble." And they said, "No, the teacher is even a former foster child. He knows how to handle them."

Turns out they put all foster kids in there; it was a computer designation: if the kid flagged up foster, then he or she HAD to go to this class.[1] Who thought that up? Next year we added her three brothers, so I went down to the school and raised a fuss. Not all these kids needed to be in a special class just because they were fosters.

"We can't do anything about that," they said. "You aren't the legal parent, and since they're not adopted, you can't sign their IEP [individualized education plan]. The real parent has to do that." So I went to DSS and asked, Is that true? All those classes we took, all that paperwork—it controlled the medical and dental and emergency needs for the kids but

not their educations? True. The school wouldn't talk to anyone but the birth parents.

"Fine, give me that form," I said. The school said, "That ain't gonna happen." But I pestered them until they did, then called DSS: "I'm taking the IEPs to be signed by the birth parents. If you never hear from me again, that's the last place anyone saw me alive." And they said, "Don't do that; you can't." And I said, "Well, you're too late, I'm calling from their driveway."

I told them [the parents] that the kids needed the best schooling they could get, and they weren't gonna get it unless they signed the form. And they signed it on the trunk of my car. I made eight or ten photocopies, then I took it back to the school and said, "Now you file this and let's talk IEP plans."

Her brothers didn't all need to be in that class. You have got to be prepared to get as crazy as the laws around you; you have to be the advocate these kids have never had. Develop your abilities to take care of these legalities, by hook or by crook. It takes a lot more time than normal parenting because you never had to do this with your kids. My kids are grown now, and we were ready to do it all again—well, once my husband talked me into it. That's why I quit my job, because keeping up with all their needs takes so much time.

One more thing. To hear "real parent" coming out of that school secretary's mouth, that about burned me as much as anything.

—foster and adoptive mom

BECKY AND her husband, Sam, are the kind of parents social workers hope for when they think of humble, teachable empty nesters ready to do good in the world. Remember that enigmatic comment Cody made in the parking lot back when we began this project, to the effect that foster parents soon realize the best way to make a difference is to choose one child or sibling group and adopt, rather than foster long-term? Sam and Becky's experiences with DSS echo that statement. The couple were parents to four bio children before they began fostering, and their oldest by birth was thirty when they started the second round. Sam pastors a small church that includes a jail ministry, and he grew up in a family that fostered. One day, Sam spoke to Becky about something he felt God had laid on his heart.

Sam's parents had taken in several kids, some short-term, some adopted. He wanted to know how Becky felt about following this path.

"I knew nothing about this whole foster thing, except that Sam's family had done it," Becky says. "I can't say it was out of the blue, but then the day comes that you decide once and for all, and go forward."

Becky and Sam queried their biological children, the two oldest married with young families, a third in college, the last one still at home: twelve-year-old Sally of the permanent smile. She is a naturally ebullient girl.

They all said, "Go for it."

Because Sally would be the biological child most affected, Becky laid down an edict she learned from talking with other foster parents: none of the new children could be older than their bio youngest. (This is advice that many foster and adoptive parents give to newbies: do not take in a foster child older than the youngest child still in your home; it prevents many troublesome dynamics.)

"I didn't want to deal with teenagers in the house when we were just getting to where we were guiding Sally through that point in life. She is a sweet, innocent child, and Sam knew what kind of lives these kids came from. We didn't want Sally exposed to anything before she was old enough to understand it."

Becky and Sam belong to a branch of Christianity that people recognize by their clothing choices, so the couple had some concerns that their religious affiliation would interfere with their fostering goals. It didn't, although the rules were made clear: they couldn't homeschool or force a foster child to attend church. It was not okay to push their beliefs on the children as rules of the household. Requiring them to read the Bible on their own as part of a daily routine was out, although family devotions were fine. For the most part, the people who helped them get licensed were not just sympathetic but downright encouraging about the Christian structure in their household.

"Structure and safety were the words I heard over and over again, in the classes and from other parents. A couple of the caseworkers said to me privately, they thought our family devotions fell right into that category," Becky says.

Becky hadn't known about the classes; back when Sam's family had fostered, they hadn't been required. She also didn't know how arduous the licensing process would be; even Sam was surprised by the new procedures. The couple didn't mind, understanding the purpose behind them, but a family medical crisis put fostering plans on temporary hold, and in the meantime, their application was lost. Sam and Becky had to start the whole process over again. Before and after that hiatus came a flurry of paperwork, home visits, and night classes.

What's covered in those classes? Keep your meds and cleaners and knives locked up. Cuddling must be initiated by the child and should also be stopped the instant the child moves away from the cuddle. Discipline and boundaries are important but cannot involve food, any form of touching, physical labor, or yelling things like "You're gonna end up just like your mother!" Twenty-four separate documents would be collected, including proof of inoculation for all household pets and a written emergency-preparedness plan in case of tornado or terrorist attack. An equipment checklist held seventeen items, among them a medication lock box, battery-operated flashlights, fans or air conditioning, and locked screens on the windows of the child's room (but no locks on the door).

It takes time to get through the application process. Two years after the "go for it" family consensus, Sam and Becky took in their first foster kids: a boy aged three and his sister, four. This was something of a test drive, as the children had an aunt who wanted custody but needed time to rearrange her housing and organize school plans. Becky and Sam took the pair believing they'd be staying only a month (which stretched to two).

Becky assumed that would become the pattern: take in temporary fosters, help them reunite with parents or extended family, and then move on to the next group. While she had them, she would invest in the children, teach them to make good life choices, instill morals, and offer stable, unconditional love. Lofty goals, but Becky took practical steps toward them, attending every class, training session, and support group or seminar she could find. She kept Sam abreast of new developments but became the primary learner and caregiver.

"I really think that's what makes good foster parents: education and an honest desire to invest in these kids' lives. You have to educate yourself, keep up with everything, and don't ever plan to have a kick-back day. It's not a piece of cake by any means, but it is rewarding. Education is the key, though. You can't ever stop learning or coming up with, like, creative ways to be the parent your kids need for as long as they need you."

Because their house had three empty bedrooms, Sam and Becky were a caseworker's dream for keeping sibling groups together. It is hard to find foster homes willing to take more than two children at a time, so the phone rang almost daily.

"It broke my heart, the needs out there." Becky's voice gets high and tight.

But with the very next group, their temporary-foster-care plan went out the window. They took in siblings ranging in age from seventeen months to five years: two boys, two girls. The children had baggage, and not just the kind that came in black garbage bags.

The term *sexualized* is used to describe kids who have witnessed or participated in sexual activities to the point that their behavior is considered inappropriate for their age. "Wise beyond their years in an unhappy way" might have described Becky and Sam's new kids. Sam and Becky expected to foster this group until their mother got help with her addiction and proved herself competent to look after them. They had been assured she was actively pursuing this goal, and their motivation to make the family whole again matched the DSS family management plan that was in place.

Instead, Becky soon felt caught between sympathy for their drug-addicted mom struggling to break free, and her own need to be trusted by the kids as weeks turned into months. She knew from experience how narrow the windows are for a baby to bond or for a child's personality to form. "Family first" had always been the couple's motto; they envisioned a holistic family-oriented ministry in which they helped the kids while others with addiction counseling experience supported the parents, until the family could reunite to live as God intended.

Yet as time progressed, Becky watched their mother disappoint, forget, ignore, and betray her children's trust. Becky began to question whether the best result ended in a return to family or guaranteed stability. Finally, she queried her allegiance to a system that focused on "everyone but the kids" and wondered how the kids could trust her when she kept following the system's mandate to allow their mom to see them no matter what her toxicity level.

"We went from praying for the family's healing, which meant Mom getting off drugs and getting her babies back, to praying that the children's healing would include understanding they couldn't live with her anymore, even though they still loved her."

Becky still remembers the day she reached the breaking point. After a particularly difficult court-ordered visit with Mom, who showed up high and ignored her children for most of it, Becky's frustration formed into one clear thought: *You don't deserve your children anymore. You have crossed the line from "I can't do this" to "I don't want to do this." How many chances have you blown? They gave you everything, a place to live, jobs, a chance to go back to school. And you have blown it all, over and over again.*

Cornering the children's caseworker and their ad litem before a hearing, she let them know in no uncertain terms how she viewed the situation. What was happening not only didn't serve the children's best interests, it felt cruel to Becky to force participation in what seemed more like a charade with each successive month. Rather than having reunification as one goal among many options, Becky felt the whole system sloped toward the parents, giving them more chances than the children's hearts could bear. Worse, this gut-twisting drama served no purpose and had no deadline for ending.

Becky decided she was done with all that. "I told the caseworker I wouldn't take the kids to any more appointments where they had to sit there wondering if their mother would show up, and go home disappointed because she didn't. Or where they were all ecstatic because she came, but then she passed out headfirst onto the table right there in front of them."

She also said one more thing that may have triggered what happened next. She let the social worker know that she and her husband were willing to adopt the four kids together. That hadn't been the plan, and Becky isn't sure if it hastened the severance of parental rights, but insiders say it almost certainly did. Caseworkers and ad litems alike are reluctant to terminate a parent's rights unless the children have a home prepared to take them, and in some states it's illegal to terminate parental rights without an adoption pending. Becky and Sam provided a ready-made solution.

This unexpected turn of events came about solely for the children's sake, Becky stresses; they hadn't been planning to adopt. "It would have just been pathetic and silly, all that back and forth with court-ordered visits, if it hadn't been really important in the lives of these babies. You can't let that kind of insanity continue to rip at any kids, anywhere, if it's in your power to stop it."

As a result of this approach, the family with four kids became a family with eight kids. A second group of siblings came to live with them a couple of years later, when Sam and the older boys put on a two-bedroom extension to the family home. This was preplanned; once the youngest of the first group went into preschool, the family thought it feasible to add a few more to the care list. It wasn't as though Becky had to do it all herself, she adds.

"Sally was such a help to me. She was fourteen by then, and she became a second mother to everybody. Diapers and feeding, and playing whatever games they wanted. She was so sweet, and they really took to her. With that much help, I felt we could manage a couple more."

Sam had barely finished the walls on the extension when the phone rang to ask if they would take in three siblings, the youngest aged two. Becky and Sam soon parented a stair-step family, with children aged three, four, five, six, eight, eight, nine, and fourteen in the house (and twenty-one, twenty-seven, and thirty-two launched out of it). In a sweet twist of fate, all the birthdays fall between April and August, "so summer at our house is one long birthday party."

Becky and Sam have already seen three children through the teen years. She knows how difficult this time is for kids and parents alike. You can train up a child in the way he or she should go, but going that way rests with him or her. Becky and Sam "pray, guide, and set boundaries." But partly because of Sam's childhood experiences, partly from his prison ministry, and in large measure due to Becky's avid soaking up of the foster-parenting classes, the couple grasped a crucial fact about those boundaries and rules that separated them from the "change the world" approach social workers so often dread: they didn't expect to parent their adopted children the way they had themselves been raised, or the way they had shepherded their first family. That's the difference Cody talked about when I first asked him about "empty nesters," and Becky grasped the difference right away.

"These kids are different from my birth children—not in a bad way; I don't mean favoritism—but in what they've seen, what they've been through, what they think the world is like. They get better as they grow older, but they have hard trust issues. My five-year-old, my husband said the other day, 'Have you noticed how in a crowd he won't interact with anyone, just stays really close to you or me?' He does; he clings to my legs sometimes when we're out shopping."

All the adoptees had nightmares, something the couple rarely saw in their bio family. Every night of the week, for weeks on end, nightmares. Even the seventeen-month-old, preverbal in the ability to express fear, exhibited it nonverbally. It stood to reason that the rules had to be enforced differently for the second family than for the first.

"My first kids always knew they were safe and loved; they were secure. These kids didn't. They'd seen so much that starting off with rules the same way I did with my kids wouldn't work. You have to meet them where they are, if you see what I mean."

Reward systems and praise are big elements of this new parenting style. Not yelling when they yell at her. Knowing when to carry someone in an appropriate way to his room when he flies out of control, so he can do no harm to self or others. Constant creativity in thinking how to help the child, not just to stop what's inappropriate now but to overcome their doing it in the future. Without ever taking anything personally.

"You have to be ready when they hit you, swear at you, scream you're not really their mom, you're not the boss. There has to be consistency, but also consequences they can understand. Honestly, it's like there are more rules for everything, things my first kids didn't need rules for, but the consequences are lighter for them. It's kind of hard to explain."

Becky knows that her second-family members never stop looking for the magic button that will cause her and Sam to say, "Nope, forget it, you've gone too far."

"There isn't one," she says. "You don't get to return your bio kids. When we adopted them, they became ours, nobody's but ours, no one's responsibility but ours. My earlier kids, I could kind of see what was coming if like an emotional storm was gathering. My second round, they blow up without warning. Some memory gets hold of them, and they panic. They can't get punished for that, but they have to know how to get out of it when it happens. And that they're safe, no matter what."

The licensing agreement and classes tightly prescribe how one physically interacts with a foster or adopted child. Not only is corporal punishment out, but fast thinking is necessary too, as on the day Becky entered the living room to find nine-year-old Ben bouncing on top of his eight-year-old foster sister Belle, simulating sex.

"You can't just haul him off. The way he sees it, they're just playing. You can't react out of your own, not like beliefs, but your own worries over a little kid knowing that much already. You have to get him off her, but you can't scare them, or hurt Ben or touch him the wrong way or make it seem like a big deal."

Becky removed the bouncing child from Belle with a suggestion that he play outdoors, and—as is required by law—she told his therapist on their next visit. A day later, CPS knocked on her door. Belle's rights may have been violated, they informed her, and they needed to talk with Belle to determine whether the incident constituted sexual molestation.

Tempest in a teapot though this turned out to be, Sam pastors a church in a small town. The couple are aware that foster parents rank just behind spiritual leaders as a favorite target for gossip.

"Our church is really supportive. When I was in the hospital a couple months ago, they cooked for the kids. They spoil them when the kids go to church—which we never had a problem with any of them wanting to do, since they came so young. Plus, if I worried about what people thought of me all the time, I'd never get anything done. This is my job. I need to do it well, and that's about the kids, not me. But I will tell you, CPS has been out here four times, always because I did what the classes told me to and reported it every time the kids acted out inappropriately over sexual behavior. Even like the little stuff. It's gotten kind of tempting to not do that anymore. I mean, let's get real, these kids are approaching the teen years."

Because of the age spread among their children, Becky and Sam will soon parent seven teens for twelve years straight.

"We're not really looking forward to that," Becky says with a sigh.

While they don't look forward to the rebellion, the real and age-appropriate sexual exploration, the boundary testing and talking back that are part of any teen's years, the thing they dread most is what to say when the kids ask about their bio parents. When a child is younger, she accepts the explanation that her mother is sick and needs to be looked after, that she can't take care of anyone else right now. But in their small town, the children's bio fathers have extended families. Eventually, the kids will be contacted again without Becky's knowledge. It's already happened once with one of the birth fathers, and Becky went head-to-head with the paternal grandparents to sever the contact. Although such contact is illegal, it's also inevitable in the social-media age. Facebook is not a foster parent's friend.

Contact notwithstanding, Becky and Sam have agreed that they will answer queries about bio parents honestly as the questions deepen with the children's teen years. They will not volunteer information but will tell what they know when asked. Sometimes at night, Becky and Sam take turns role-playing as the kids asking questions, trying to give the background facts without taking sides or adding drama and opinion. Becky also knows that, when they are old enough to drive, odds are good her children will go look up their birth moms without telling her—and that the community will be only too happy to report this back to her and Sam. She doesn't have a problem with that, either; she sees their job as providing a safe place and a chance to practice making good choices. But she does pray often for God to protect her kids from unintended consequences when they start looking for their birth moms.

"When we adopted them, we made a covenant to equip these kids for life. Safety and structure—it's my job to give these things to them. Their lives have a little extra baggage going on, and that's part of what I have to get them ready to face. It's not my place to say they shouldn't go find their birth moms. It's my place to help them understand what else they discover when they find her, and make good decisions after that."

With all that to deal with now and look forward to later, why do they foster? Becky doesn't hesitate.

"When I asked my oldest son what he thought about us doing this, he said, 'Who's going to help those kids if not you, Mom?' It's very fulfilling, but don't get the wrong idea, because it's also a lot of work. Lots of stress, lots of emotion, lots of redirecting what you were taught into different channels—not changing your morals, but redirecting how you get your point across. Staying focused on the kids. Always on the kids. You never get to just kick back; you have to deal with every day on a day-by-day basis. But it is rewarding.

"Ben, my nine-year-old, he sometimes gets aggressive, leaves bruises on me, and the other day, you know what he said to me? He said, 'Mom, you are the best mom, better than my other mom ever was. Thanks for helping me.' And that hits you right in the heart. You're having an impact on their life. That makes it all worth it."

Becky is not known personally to Dale, but when he hears her story, he grins. "See? There's still some inspiration in the world. And plenty of compassionate people. That's what it's all about."

6

For Love or Money

I'm one of the only licensed clinical social workers in this area—there might be five of us—which means I've probably counseled or assessed or been guardian ad litem for half the foster families in this county. I'd say 70 percent of them are in it for the money.

They're easy to spot. You see a woman with five foster teens driving a fancy car wearing a Rolex, you know you're looking at a paycheck parent. Those girls don't have designer purses, but Mama does.

I tried to bust her. She's got all her kids on psychotropic drugs for "anxiety," but they're not taking those Xanax and lithium prescriptions. She's selling them. Her oldest foster daughter helps with the sales at the high school; the others just hand over their pills. Plus there's the monthly stipends—five, all for teens, all in therapeutic care.

Add it up: the teen therapeutic stipend times five, so that's about $9,000, plus the drug money. I'm not even gonna try reckoning that up for you. Per month. Tax free.

I refused to support prescriptions for those girls, so they went to another LCSW. The investigation was inconclusive. I don't know that I expected anything else. I just had to try.

I tell you, I'm suspicious of any foster home that has more than one teen at a time, unless they're siblings. I'm raising two teenagers right now,

and there isn't enough money in the world to make me deal with their shit
for anything other than pure blind love.

—Cassie, LCSW

We had this one couple, and they came in and said, "We need you to
pay for one of our foster daughters to go to counseling." "What kind of
counseling?" we said. "She thinks she's a lesbian. She's only thirteen.
She's confused from all that's happened to her in the system." This was
a sexualized kid. The mom had looked up some places that could counsel
people not to be gay. We couldn't pay for that. When I told her so, this
mom, who I think genuinely loved this kid, she said, "Well, I'm not having this in my house. She could harm the other girls, talking to them. You
have to move her. We love her, but she can't stay." We did. I tried not to
judge this woman, but part of me still thinks, If you thought being gay
would send you to Hell, and you loved somebody, if the system
told you that you couldn't have money to "cure" her, wouldn't you
spend your own? *These people had seven foster kids. They weren't hurt-*
ing, either. I don't know. Anyway, we aren't in the business of talking kids
out of being gay. Or into it.

—therapeutic social worker

WHEN PEOPLE uninvolved in foster care learned I was writing a book on the
subject, sooner or later, one of them would ask a question about money.
As in, how many parents are doing it just for the money? Likewise, the social workers I interviewed vented serious fury on the "paycheck parents"[1]
who were taking advantage of the system—although I found it interesting
that these parents weren't their first complaint. Social workers talked most
about parents who thought they knew it all and thus blew their responses
to children in need. The general public asked about the parents who were
exploiting the system.

It's a sad truth that, while what makes everything worthwhile to some is
the impact they might have on a child's life, others find fulfillment in what

they see as a paycheck. Dale gets annoyed when people use that word to refer to the payments given to foster parents. He reminds everyone that the funding is, in fact, a stipend intended to cover what the family spends on the child. "That money belongs to the child and is given in trust to his or her foster parents. When people start talking about it as a paycheck, they're already on the wrong mental track."

Now would be a good time to explain that fostering and adopting from the state or from a therapeutic agency contracted with the state does not cost anything. Through a complicated system that varies both by state and according to the specific needs of the child, an assessment is made as to what payment per month needs to be available for his care.[2] These payments may not stop when the child is adopted, a fact that seems to startle the general public the first time they hear it; if the child has needs that will continue over the long term, as is most often the case in therapeutic care, parents continue to receive a stipend after her adoption.

All foster kids receive Medicaid, free school lunch and breakfast, and additional payments as needed for counseling support, but therapeutic placements receive about triple the stipend of regular foster care, no matter the age of the kid. (A Virginia teen in regular care would receive $671 monthly, compared to a therapeutic teen's $1,800.) Although that tripled money is a blatant attempt to attract homes for hard-to-place kids, it is also to pay for the additional burdens associated with their care. Among the other extra duties that come with medical fragility, learning disabilities, or behavioral issues that may have contributed to or resulted from the children's bouncing between homes, therapeutic foster parents do nightly paperwork, including a report sheet documenting activities, medicines, therapy, and any behavioral incidents. Regular foster parents are meant to do a weekly review.

In therapeutic care, accountability for what's spent is higher. DSS does issue guidelines for regular care, but receipts to prove that purchases have been made are rarely required. For the private agencies providing therapeutic care, parents must show that they spent—with variance between states—about $110 per month on clothing, $90 on recreation (magazine subscriptions, after-school classes, sports equipment, whatever the youngster is interested in), and a minimum of $30 for a teen's pocket money.

The rest of the stipend is to be used for appointments, gas money for driving to said appointments, and the all-important savings account for

when the adopted or permanent-placement foster child turns eighteen and
the family has no further legal obligation to him.

Cody is quick to condemn on this last point because, he says, he and his
colleagues rarely see it handled well. "That's the child's money. Supposed
be put in the bank against college or a car or getting started in life when
they graduate. Would you like to know how many foster homes do that?
No, you wouldn't."

Dale makes a good point when he asserts that the funding is not a paycheck to the parent for providing care but a stipend with which to provide
what the child needs. Yet the sad naked truth is that discerning who is motivated more by money than by altruism may not matter all that much to
those fighting the good fight.

Stories abound in every part of the United States of people filling their
homes with kids rather than love; it's not considered unusual. Here in
Coalton, caseworkers, ad litems, and a few other key players estimate that
those taking advantage of funding to supplement their own income make
up a frightening number of foster homes. Cody and Beth said half. Cassie
reckoned "at least" 70 percent. Dale, after a pained silence, offered, "Thirty
percent, tops."[3]

"When you mix up human emotions, money, kids, and public opinion,
you're asking for it. And that's exactly what the foster care system has done
on this subject," says Cody.

LCSW Cassie was pretty succinct in the interview when fostering for
monetary reasons came up. We were in the classics room of my bookstore,
and when I asked about funding, she stood and closed the door before answering. In essence, she said, those "bilking the system" are taking up a lot
of public bandwidth but are not the biggest problem for social workers;
getting rid of truly abusive homes—that is, identifying and eliminating
those that slip through the licensing process undetected—is their priority.

"There are some real stinkers out there, but most of these edgy homes
are just people trying to make do, and maybe trying to be good to somebody. The system can weed out the really bad apples. But the mediocre
ones—my impression has been that it can't afford to weed them out." Cassie shrugged, her mouth a thin line.

By "mediocre" she means those homes where the basic physical needs
of the children are met and no one is suffering deliberate physical or verbal

abuse, yet the children are not treated with affection or love, nor are their stipends spent primarily on their needs.

To a casual observer like me, DSS workers seem to rank motivation far lower in the placement criteria than availability. After my conversation with Cassie, who is a counselor and sometimes ad litem rather than a social worker with a caseload to manage, it took weeks to get any of the social workers to engage with the question: why are kids left in foster homes that common sense would suggest are in it for the money?

Finally, perhaps grudgingly, a consensus statement emerged, honed by edits from repeated interviews: *Not even the worst social worker in Coalton or anywhere else would knowingly send a child to an unsafe home, but a mediocre placement is better than leaving the child in a volatile situation. It is a matter of degrees, and there's no way to discuss the bad-mediocre-good continuum in a polite manner without fallout—like discussing whether the kids should be taken from the home in the first place versus what could happen to them in care—so we [social workers] prefer not to engage with it.*

In fact, Cody takes issue with my phrasing of the question. He points out two inherent assumptions. First, a home fostering for the money might not be a bad home. Stability and safety are the primary needs for a foster child; if someone sees the money given for the care of the child in their home as a paycheck rather than as a stipend for that child's care, the "good versus bad" dividing line depends on how well the child's needs are being met. Not to mention that people's motivations can shift over time; proximity can create fertile soil for affection to blossom, so what starts as a job might end in love.

Second, Cody feels that asking why social workers don't weed out and close such homes suggests that social workers are the driving force and deciding factor, when home availability is the real determinant. Cody sees a circular blame game surrounding that not-fantastic home: the public blames social workers for being too lazy (or otherwise unwilling) to complete the machinations required to move a child from it; social workers blame the public who could afford to foster without those hefty payments they are so quick to decry for being too lazy (or otherwise unwilling) to become foster parents.

"People think we're using bad homes because we don't care? Tell them to become a good foster home, and we'll call them instead. They'll see how fast we care." The harsh tone in Cody's voice could break rock.

A fifteen-year veteran of therapeutic social work, Cody recalls words of wisdom he received from Dale when he first started—Dale, the wise old grandfather social worker who began his career in DSS, then went to therapeutic care in a private agency, and then came back to a director's position in DSS "because they needed him." He stands ready to dispense advice and kick butt as needed, and many of his former employees call to talk over complex cases. As one of his protégés puts it, "Dale has seen everything twice, but he's still smiling, and he still believes in God."

Cody now directs an agency in his own right, but back when Dale was training him, one of their early hallway meetings centered around so-called "paycheck parents."

"He told me it kinda sucks to be suspicious of all those saintly people who step up to the plate and foster multiple kids, but you get used to it after a while."

One of the things foster parents, caseworkers, and the public alike agree on is that it's not a natural impulse to want to look after someone else's children. Add to that the suspicion engendered when caseworkers like Cody, Beth, and Barbie have parents pull them aside at support group meetings to ask questions like, "We measured that unfinished room in the basement, and I think we could fit bunk beds in. If I finish the walls, could we up our license to five kids? Would it need a window?" Such conversations are as common as the support group meetings at which they occur, the group agrees. Foster parents who upgrade their houses or cars can expect whispers to ripple through their neighborhoods.

Keep in mind, as you think through the issues of how to identify those taking advantage of the system for financial gain, that its employees are following the DSS guidelines for children taken into their care. First, keep the family intact; next, reunite the family, using fosters as needed; failing that, get the children adopted or permanently placed with a relative; if that's not an option, get them adopted with as few foster placements as possible; if you can't do that, get them into some safe and stable foster care situation for as long as possible.

Finding a situation that will be permanent, stable, and able to look after a young'un physically and emotionally takes time, energy, attention, and cooperation between multiple parties and an alignment in timing and moving parts. It may involve trying out a few foster homes before the fit is right—and don't forget those potential court-ordered bounces back to Bio Mom or Dad. Confounding everyone's plans could be an interested relative or two in unstable circumstances.

A regular foster care worker's average caseload across Coalton is thirty, according to Elizabeth (her maximum was thirty-seven), but those on Cody's team in therapeutic care have just seven. Therapeutic workers talk to their kids at least once a week; regular caseworkers average once per month for most, although they may track a few more often if their situation seems precarious, and most social workers have favorites they keep up with more closely as well. It is easy for a mediocre foster home to thrive when DSS workers are stretched to these limits, with no known better alternatives. Kids in regular foster care are, therefore, more likely to fall between the cracks than those in therapeutic care, or to bounce, as Cami and her sister did, because someone let up on supervision.

"I hate that phrase 'fall between the cracks,'" interjects Barbie, the spitfire newcomer, as I outline my understanding of reasons why "bad" homes might still be used in the system. "Children do not fall between cracks. They fall down because somebody let them down. We're all busy. We're all overworked and underpaid. But if we let something slide, that's not 'falling between the cracks.' That's us failing a child we're paid to help."

Cody swings between sympathy for and frustration with his DSS colleagues. He talks about his visit to a home after the foster mother there called about a child, aged fifteen, who was having medical issues. "Cattle Farm" is the cynical nickname caseworkers use among themselves for this infamous home. Only teens pass through the place, and the matriarch, a whip-thin woman whose word is law, refers to herself as "the Boss."

Primarily a regular foster home, the Cattle Farm hosted three brothers; we can call them Stuart, Colin, and Ewan. Colin was in therapeutic care due to medical fragility. His older brother Stuart had developed a stomach condition. After the foster mom made a few calls to say that Stuart wasn't eating and she was concerned, the social worker who had placed most of the children there asked Cody to take Stuart to a doctor's appointment. He wanted Cody to do the transport and simultaneously assess the need to move the teen from regular to therapeutic care due to his stomach difficulties. The way Cody heard it, the lad would stay in the home but change categories.

"Now remember, this is considered a good family." Cody leans forward, props an elbow on his office desk, and wags a finger with the skill of a natural storyteller, narrowing his eyes as he resumes. "Six adopted teenagers live in this house, plus the foster kids, and this is a place DSS can call at 3:00 a.m., and the Boss will take them. Teenagers only. She won't take anybody under age twelve."

Cody pulled up in front of a big, sprawling, ranch-style home. In the driveway, he met the family patriarch, head stuck under the hood of an antique truck. He answered Cody's greeting, learned what he wanted, and pointed toward the house with his wrench.

"She takes care of all that. In there. I keep out of it."

Heads up, thought Cody. Only one parent involved in a two-parent family is a big red flag for caseworkers.

On the porch, Stuart was waiting. "Ready for your appointment?" Cody asked, but Stuart blinked at him, his eyes registering confusion.

The Boss appeared at the screen door, beckoning. "Could I see you inside, please?"

As he passed Stuart, Cody realized the young man stood next to a black garbage bag, about two-thirds full.

Uh-oh.

The Boss came swiftly to the point. "We thought you were coming to get him for good. That's what I told the caseworker to ask you to do. He doesn't fit in here, won't eat what I fix. He doesn't like being here. He isn't a good fit for our family. I got two boys coming in the morning, and they're going to need that bunk bed."

Cody nodded. "Looks like there's been a miscommunication. Lemme go ahead and take Stuart to the doctor, and then I'll talk to his caseworker, and maybe we can swing back by to collect his stuff."

In the car, Cody was barely out of the driveway when Stuart asked, "You mind taking me to Hardee's? I'm hungry."

After the drive-through, Cody watched Stuart consume an upsized burger and fries with a large soda, then drawled, "The Boss tells me you won't eat."

Stuart shrugged.

"That's not giving me any information, buddy. You talk to your caseworker about your stomach condition?"

Silence.

"Clears that up," said Cody. "Tell me about the other kids in the house, what're they like?"

Stuart rolled down his window.

"What are their names?"

"Dunno."

"You don't know? Didn't you ever ask?"

"She doesn't encourage us to talk a lot. Me and my brothers share a room. I don't know the other boys; I think there's two, but one's always working someplace. Three girls share a room, and her daughter has her own."

They drove in silence to the doctor. While Stuart was inside, Cody called his caseworker, a man he describes as "a sorry-ass shoe-shopper." (That's a nickname for caseworkers who do not spend their working hours on work. For some reason, Cody uses new shoes against CPS employees the way others attach donuts to cops.)

"What gives with the Farm?" Cody asked without preamble.

The sigh on the other end was audible. "Listen, Cody, classify him as medically fragile, and get that kid outta there and into therapeutic care where he belongs. He's messing up my good foster home with these people. I got six permanent placements outta them so far, plus a lot more difficult placements. Maybe they'll keep him if he gets therapeutic payments, even after the trouble he's caused. If he doesn't want to be there, I could use the place for someone who'd appreciate it. Although he should appreciate it, since we worked hard to keep him and his brothers together."

"What's the deal with his not eating? He was ready to eat my dashboard when I picked him up."

"She's one of those old schoolers. The kids stay at the table until they've eaten everything on their plate. Apparently, one time they had green beans, and he didn't finish, and he had to stay there until he did, and ever since then it's been a little messed up at dinnertime. With this kid's stomach condition, he should be in a therapeutic home."

Cody cast his mind back to the Cattle Farm. The kitchen door had been closed, but he was building a pretty good idea about what he'd find behind it. He planned to confirm on their return. Stuart emerged from the doctor's office with a prescription and a suggestion that he "eat more, and take it slowly. Just relax and chew." On the way back to the house, he asked Cody to slow down.

"You worried about going back?" Cody didn't take his eyes off the road.

"A little." The boy's voice registered something between resignation and apprehension.

"What's this I hear about you being stubborn over some green beans?"

Stuart stiffened. "She cooks beans and taters. Well, the girls do. My brother likes green beans. I don't."

"That the only thing you won't eat?"

After a pause, Stuart said, "She feeds us beans and taters about five nights a week. Sometimes meatloaf, sometimes chicken. But mostly, beans and taters."

Cody nodded. "Canned beans?"

Stuart glanced at him, then away. "Home canned, not the kind from the store."

"Girls doing the canning?"

This time Stuart didn't say anything, just cut his eyes to Cody's hands on the steering wheel, then back to the windshield.

Cody tried again. "What kind of chores you do indoors?"

Stuart remained silent. Cody wasn't surprised. Experience had taught him that a foster child wound up trying to manipulate his caseworker one conversation in five. By sneakiness or straight-out asking, almost always the kids wanted something—fast food, maybe to move houses, even just to be told their hair looked nice or their clothes were cool. And he'd learned early in the job that, the more they really needed the thing they wanted, the quieter they tended to be when asking for it.

"God gave social workers superpowers for a reason," Dale often tells his team at staff meetings. "One is observation; the other is anticipation. Use these for the greater good, and put out the fires before they start."

Back at the Cattle Farm, Cody asked for a glass of iced tea. One of the girls fetched it for him, but he followed her back to the sparkling clean kitchen where two more girls worked, one stirring two large pots, the other scrubbing a sink.

Six feet tall and blue-eyed, Cody turned on his considerable charm. "This place looks amazing!" he said. "Bet y'all are great cooks!"

One of the girls smiled. "Homemade. Would you like some?" She spooned up a ladle full of beans and potatoes, which smelled delicious, and dumped them on a saucer.

"Little bit of bacon for seasoning?" Cody asked. "My wife makes hers that way."

The girl giggled. "Go on, see whose are better."

He took the dish with a smile. "Gotta admit, these're pretty good, but you can't make me dis my wife's cooking."

All the girls laughed. Cody pronounced the beans delicious, handed back the saucer, and went back to the living room, where the Boss sat watching a boy in his teens dust. Since he resembled Stuart, Cody assumed it was Ewan.

"You asked about Stuart going to another placement," he said, and the boy glanced up.

The Boss answered. "That child is such a picky eater. I'm sure it's got to do with his ulcer, I understand that, but I can't have him disrupting meal-times at my house. I've had to sit hours with him until he finished his food. We can't have that kind of unruliness here. With these kids, you know, it's impossible to let anyone get away with that kind of stubbornness."

Cody nodded, taking in the immaculate front room. Every armchair had doily slipcovers, the flat-screen TV free of dust. "Where are the other kids now?" he asked.

"My daughter's in there with, you know, my other daughters. Two boys at work right now, McDonald's. They're good workers, both of them."

"I can imagine. Well, Stuart can come with me now, and I'll let you know where he goes so his brothers can know where he's at."

The Boss turned to the boy who was dusting. "If you want to say good-bye, you can knock that off a minute."

Cody waited while the brothers chatted briefly on the porch, then Stuart ran down the stairs clutching his garbage sack. In the car, he stared straight ahead.

"You sad about leaving your brothers?" Cody asked.

Stuart shrugged. After a minute, he said, as if answering a question, "She works us to death. You get home from your job, she's got chores. Get up at 6:00 a.m. and wash windows, different part of the house each week. There's a park next door; we never get any free time to go have a ball game.

It's work in the house, work your job, go to school, do your homework, work in the house, work your job. Only one of us not got a job bringing in a paycheck is Colin. She takes our pay for rent."

As a medically fragile child with a learning disability, Colin had a full-time caregiver paid for by Medicaid. The worker was assigned to Colin after school and stayed with him until 8:00 p.m. Stuart and his brother Ewan took turns assisting him to bed.

Cody kept his voice noncommittal. "Mmm. Let's see what kinda placement we can get you tonight. I got a family in mind that maybe has a bed." He did not add that the placement would move Stuart into therapeutic care and hence up his chances of staying with an emergency family that night, rather than driving to the Coal Mountain Group Home about an hour away.

"In therapeutic care?" Stuart asked, and Cody laughed.

"Y'all know the system better than we do."

Stuart's face remained expressionless. "I don't want to spend the night in a group home."

Sobering, Cody said, "I'm hoping you won't, but let's see. If you do, I will do my best to get you into this new place by tomorrow noon."

They drove in silence a moment, then Stuart said, "It wasn't the beans. Why she wanted me to leave. I'm bad at cleaning. I can't clean a bathroom to save my life. Never could seem to get the hang of it." The boy grinned.

The family was available, and Stuart went straight to them. After dropping Stuart off, Cody drove to his colleague's office, where he met the "sorry-ass shoe-shopper" coming out the door at 4:15, headed for home.

"You were able to move him?" he asked, and when Cody said so, Shopper exhaled in relief. "Good. I feel for the kid, but I can't have a sick boy messing up my best foster home."

"You know she's in it for the money and the work she gets out of those kids." Cody did not invest his words with any particular energy. It didn't seem worthwhile.

It was Shopper's turn to shrug. "Why should today be different?"

Concluding his story, Cody picks up the thread of our earlier conversation.

"People reading that, they're gonna think, 'Why didn't that sorry-ass Cody do more for those kids, get them out of that work camp?' I'll tell you why. I feel sorry for my colleagues having to make do with homes like that.

They got all those cases and not enough places. Nobody would leave a kid in a dangerous home, but that one was just sorry. And sometimes, sorry is all there is to work with.

"The kids had clothes on. Their shoes were solid, not full of holes, not held on with duct tape. Eating regular meals. Eating the same thing a lot, but their bellies were full. They had clean hair. They lived in a clean house, nobody sleeping on a pile of dirty clothes or feces. Or worse. It's out there. They were inside cleaning, not out shooting up. They had beds. Real beds.

"Yeah, she's in it for the money. She had a BMW jeep out there, and her husband had that antique souped-up truck. There was a boat around back. And there sat that old Ford Coupe the kids were sharing to get back and forth from work. She's keeping their foster money for her own stuff, plus charging them rent from their pay? Yeah, we get it.

"But where are you gonna put eight kids ages fourteen to seventeen, one of them learning disabled with a feeding tube, and he's got two brothers so they should all be together? Tell me who wants those kids more than the money for looking after them? The girls weren't scared of me as a strange man, and they were proud of their food. Nobody was physically harming them. That's not saying hard work is the cure or even appropriate in every foster situation. I'm not saying she's doing right. I am saying she's the best available right now. We can't afford to wait for good homes. We're stuck with the ones where outright bad ain't going on. Tell your readers, they don't like it, they should become foster parents."

By "we" he means social workers in general. Those who work for private agencies and those who work for the government may come to loggerheads at times, but they understand one another's challenges. Usually. Cody adds a moral to this story.

"I'm gonna say one more thing. My fellow social worker, the sorry-ass shoe-shopper? Yeah, I feel like he should've been looking for better instead of trying to get me to remove the squeaky wheel doing the complaining. But who am I to judge? I only had to place one kid. He'd've had to find homes for a bunch of teenagers. That's his job, but how many of those do you think would've been in it for the money anyway?"

The Cattle Farm is a textbook example of how age factors into foster care in difficult ways. Depending on how long it's taken for parental rights to terminate, how competent the social worker's been, and how involved the extended family became, the child in foster care who's not yet been adopted (or even been declared eligible for it) may reach an age when the goal flips from adoption to permanent foster placement.

Care staff make no bones about it: from ages zero to three, a child is so easy to place that only social etiquette prevents calling the kid a sellable commodity. This coincides with the period that child development experts consider the crucial years in which personality and worldview form. After the age of three, a child may learn to adapt, but the critical underpinnings of personal choices, reactions, and assumptions are set in something akin to mental concrete. All before the little one is even fully verbal.

"We never have enough foster parents, but when we get a new family, five will get you ten they signed up to foster an infant," Beth says with a sigh. "Or at least somebody under six."

Liz of Family Preservation Services is blunt. "You have heard of the old bait-and-switch? That describes us, my staff and me. We are masters at selling parents looking for a two-year-old girl on the joys of an immediately available six-and-a-half-year-old boy and his older sister. If I ever do give up this brilliant career, I will rake in millions as a used-car salesman."

Despite Liz's cynicism, a child from three to eight years of age or so is not such a hard sell, either. A child in this range can prove malleable, still showing the potential to form trust bonds in the minds of hopeful parents. People desperate to start a family might be willing to start in the middle of the "raising years," and DSS workers are primed to cajole them from the other end of the phone line.

"We don't share the same goals at this point, us and the foster families," says Barbie. "We're trying to get kids off the books. They're trying to find the family members they want to bond with. From our point of view, the form goes out the window."

She is referring to that infamous five-page document those fostering to adopt or provide long-term placements fill out, listing preferences on ages, sexes, personality traits, physical characteristics, and anything else one can think of. Prospective foster parents check boxes. Social workers file the papers. And then the kids who actually need help show up, and they're the wrong age, so social workers begin their siren phone calls.

Social workers describe a gap in foster homes willing to take in eight-to-twelve-year-olds. The reason for this gap is ugly. When caseworkers see a family filling its home with permanent-placement teenagers, they give one another knowing looks. That's where parents more interested in supplemental income than caring for a child tend to congregate.

The difference in the therapeutic stipend for a child aged eleven versus twelve is $300 per month; in regular foster care the difference is $100. Foster parents can take the added angst of a teen in return for additional cash, or the younger kid and maybe a little more peace and quiet, at least until puberty hits. (By the time the littl'un has become a big'un, according to the system, parent and child should have affection enough to ensure continuity—another idea that looks great on paper but plays roulette with human emotions and doesn't factor in motivations stemming from the poverty so rife throughout Coalton.) For someone who's in it for the money, it makes more sense to jump to age twelve.

Permanent placement is an alternative to adoption aimed only at those twelve and older. It's a covert admission that someone on the cusp of those dreaded teen years is too old to be attractive to adopting families in all but the rarest of circumstances; thus, finding a foster who will agree to keep the child until the age of eighteen without becoming the child's legal parent is the next best thing. The big money for fostering is at the deep end of the pool with kids over the age of twelve, and if they're in therapeutic foster care, the funding is much deeper. A psychologist who recently retired from the area agreed with Dale that the government is offering that money for what should be seen as support for the child rather than as a paycheck. Then she outlined a few observations on why it might not be perceived that way.

"[Paycheck] parents aren't self-aware. It's not a case of admitting it, but of recognizing themselves in the first place. Take the culture of the area. People are going to say I'm dealing in stereotypes. Let them. Here in the southeast part of this state we've got poverty in spades, mistrust of the government—earned mistrust is still mistrust, I'm not saying they don't deserve it for all the bullshit they've pulled on coal miners. Then we have a natural gravitation toward community and familial bonds. Family is everything here. You don't shirk your duty.

"Now translate that: Big Brother who took away your job, or your husband's job, will pay you big money to look after the kids of someone who's not morally as strong as you, who failed in their family duty and fell by the wayside. Can't you see the disconnect that results? There's no self-awareness; these schmucks think they're the best thing to happen to those poor kids. They're flooding DSS. The only reason therapeutic foster care isn't overrun by creeps looking for big payouts is that screening process."

The therapeutic stipend repays what the child has cost the household—a category that can stretch into incredulity in homes motivated by money. One can justify increases in water, electricity, and other monthly expenses. Most of these children need special counseling. Teen boys have been known to inhale $500 in groceries per month, something anyone with experience feeding growing lads can affirm. But the whole water bill, upgrades on the new swimming pool, the entire cost of the child's Christmas presents? These excesses came up at one of the group interviews I held at an agency office, and the social workers dropped pizza slices to plates, food forgotten as they fought to top one another's stories of financial abuse.

The winner was the gas grill. One family bought a top-of-the-line model, then put it under their solo foster kid's recreational costs because "we made him hamburgers on it too." In second place came receipts for tampons and toilet paper. "Oh, you didn't buy any of those before your foster child arrived?" A case worker shakes her head.

"Was their foster child a girl?" another asks, and laughter rumbles through the room.

The senior manager in attendance watches her team vent with something between dismay and affection as they vie for worst-case scenarios, then sums up this part of the interview process with an assertive voice and hand movements intended to damp down the rising hilarity. "Let's just say you could get cynical pretty fast, reviewing purchases. Can we move on now?"

Cassie is succinct when I ask her about the Cattle Farm (a place with which she is familiar).

"Here's the thing about most of the foster parents I meet: the creeps don't realize they are. Not just paycheckers. It's never just one motivation. A lot of children who were fostered or adopted become foster parents. They're planning to make it better for the next generation than they had it. Their economic circumstances tend to be unstable at best, so the money they receive for doing good—in their eyes, they've earned that.

"If you come from a chaotic home, whether you're the parent or the child, to them it's just levels of bad. If you're used to living in deep bad, and bad is a little better here, then it's an improvement. By the time they're teenagers, if they've been in the system awhile, they've learned survival techniques that don't include expecting people to care about them on an individual level."

Cassie describes a boy she used to counsel who entered one of their sessions over-the-moon excited because his foster family had taken him to get new clothes before school started. He had never had new clothes before and called the shopping trip "major cool."

"'That's great,' I said. 'Where all did you go?'"

It turns out that the parents took him to a thrift store in Walker City, paying about a third of what would have been paid new. The lad didn't care; he had new clothes. According to Cassie, the foster dad bought a sports car about three months later.

"You tell me, is that bad parenting, or good for the boy? The kid thought it was just fine. Am I supposed to disillusion him?" Cassie raises her eyebrows. "Define 'good' when it comes to a foster home. Define 'physical needs met.' Define 'emotional involvement.'"

At our next bakery lunch, Beth picks up the theme of financial versus emotional involvement with enthusiasm. The Cattle Farm may be notorious in the system, but it is not alone. Beth talks about a foster child we can call Alison, aged thirteen, who was embarrassed at eating the free breakfast at her school. Alison told Beth she'd been going without breakfast because her family didn't provide them on weekdays. They knew breakfast and lunch were free for all foster kids. Alison got a home-cooked supper but had started hoarding food, which led to a call to her caseworker. After Beth chatted with the teen and realized what was happening, her frustration with the parents boiled over.

"'Buy her a stupid Pop-Tart' was what I wanted to say. Instead, I think it came out like 'You know how easy teens are to embarrass. She doesn't want her friends at school to see her getting breakfast.' It was the way they served the kids; you couldn't pick a free-lunch recipient out of the line, but breakfast was in a separate room or something like that. You could see who got it."

Did the family buy her Pop-Tarts?

"No," Beth sighs. "Said she had to learn to accept what life gave her." She pauses and smiles without it touching her eyes. "What are Pop-Tarts, like $2.50 a box?"

At our next meeting, which happens to be at my bookstore rather than his office, Dale listens to me outline the stories of the Cattle Farm, Alison, the thrift-store shopping trip. He rolls his eyes at the feeding frenzy culminating in the gas-grill story and sighs. Then he leans forward, thudding his glass of water to the table, and looks me in the eye. A mild-mannered, articulate man with graying temples, Dale wears suits to work. Yet he still gives the impression that he is about to adjust his white cowboy hat and fire with deadeye aim.

"If you're doing it right as a foster parent, you won't make money, but you won't be out of pocket for much, either. That's supposed to be the point of how needs for the kids are assessed and valued for payout, this balance somewhere in the middle where the pendulum won't swing quite so much. You have to draw a distinction in a rural area. Think about it. There are people who won't foster unless they get paid, as they see it, but then around here there are an awful lot of people, good people, who can't afford to foster unless they get something to foster with. Sure, we hear a lot about how awful some are, but we don't see those people so quick to condemn stepping in to take up the slack. They can criticize when they're ready to become foster parents and do them one better. We're waiting."

He sits back, takes a sip of water, and gives me a smile.

"How's that for an inspirational quote? That oughta bring 'em in."

7

What's Love Got to Do with It?

Fostering is hard, but it isn't impossible, or only for saints. Everybody knows foster parents need to be patient and understanding. But also, they should be financially stable. You can't be a good foster parent if you can't look after yourself without the money you'll get for fostering. That's meant to be spent on us and if you're really going to be our parent, you're going to spend it all. Do the math before you start so you don't get sucked in.

Next, have a support system. Get one if you don't have one, before you start. Otherwise you will rip your hair out. If you can't share what's going on, go home and cry to somebody, if there's no support system, don't be in there. Don't start without one. You'll give up and that's not going to help anybody.

And then, as much as people talk about money, they should talk about time. Kids don't just need to be emotionally invested in like "Hi how was your day that's nice" but to have time invested in us too. Foster parents need to teach us things we should've learned already. Things I should have learned when I was a little kid I'm just learning now, when I'm in college. Almost every kid in the system is delayed in some area, so there are all these things we should know but don't. You need to really think if you have time for us; I mean, we're not like a puppy but we need some training.

—e-mail from a former foster child

DESPITE THE intense cynicism exhibited by so many inside and outside of the system, Dale believes most parents foster for better reasons than a paycheck. So does Marilyn, a former foster child, but she adds an interesting twist to the concept.

Now in her twenties, Marilyn aged out of foster care after a failed adoption[1] at the age of fourteen sent her to a group home. She lives in University City, although the people who adopted her live in the community of Little Stony Creek, not far from the holler where Kim grew up amid her tangled family. Unlike Kim, Marilyn was not surrounded by relatives; she grew up in a foster home of a different race to hers, practically the only person of her ethnicity in Little Stony.

As an adult looking back on her own childhood while working with children like herself, Marilyn observes that sometimes foster parents get confused when children aren't as ready to bond as the parents hoped; when a feel-good kickback from doing what is right fails to appear, parents may feel a bit more entitled to and appreciative of payment. People who believe they will love and be loved "faster than a foster kid can keep up" can come to see the child as their responsibility but not their joy once they realize their foster kids might be too wary to trust their good intentions. Or too damaged to bond.

"I'm in a private online support group for former foster kids. You'd be surprised how many of us had that conversation when we were twelve, fourteen, when your parents who adopted you sit you down and say, 'It's obvious you never loved us. That's okay, but we're going to let you go.' Like, what does a twelve-year-old whose parents abandoned you know about love?"

They know more about broken promises, Marilyn says. I ask her what it felt like to hear such reasoning when she had thought herself "adopted and safe." She gives me an enigmatic look, something between guarded and exasperated.

"It felt like the thing that was always gonna happen. Someday the shoe would drop, and this promise would get broken too. I say that now, as a healthy grown woman looking back on what happened then, but at the time, it was just words that meant 'pack your stuff up, honey; you're moving on again.' I was never really not expecting that."

Sometimes parents persevere even after they find their foster child isn't going to return their emotional investment as quickly or with as much interest as they had hoped. Foster parent and child psychologist Sharon is one example, but I didn't interview her; her colleague Lila told me about Sharon. Lila is a longtime friend of mine and a therapist who works primarily with teens. Though they are business partners in their clinical practice, neither Sharon nor Lila practices in Coalton. At the age of seven, Judith came to live with Sharon, and following involuntary termination of Judith's mother's rights (Judith's father was dead), Sharon adopted her.

Sharon had seen many foster children in her practice and talked often with Lila about how they should each take on a foster child. About to marry a man with four teenage children, Lila declined. Sharon pursued licensure as a foster parent on her own.

"I'd say they were fairly delighted to see her, what with her background," Lila observes with dry humor. "I think she got Judith like the day after her license came."

Judith came from an abusive background. She had witnessed her father's violent death. Her mother, a substance abuser, had from an early age left the little girl locked alone in their apartment. Sharon knew that "Judith would never be a loving, cuddly child. She wasn't expecting that. I don't know if DSS sent her a hard case because they knew she could handle it. What I do know is Sharon understands that Judith is damaged for life. She isn't going to bond. She uses the word *job* to describe being Judith's adoptive mom."

Lila adds in a firm and swift coda that she doesn't mean Sharon is adopting Judith for any reason other than love. "She cares about Judith's well-being and takes her places and makes sure she's clothed and fed and looks out for her. She invests in her emotionally without expecting a return—which is exhausting as a therapist, so I can't imagine what it would be like as a mom. She teaches her things she needs to know to live a comfortable life. And she knows Judith won't be able to love her back, [so it's] not a lifelong bond. She doesn't kiss Judith goodnight or hug her because Judith doesn't want her to. And she's okay with that. Do you want me to define whether that's love or not, not expecting anything back from the person you're giving to?"

Some parents do indeed tough it out and give without expectation of return. Others expect more, one way or another. After the classes required to get a license these days, Dale adds, no one can be in doubt as to the emotional baggage kids who have been bouncing through the system are likely to carry.

"That's why they like babies so much." Dale doesn't even crack a smile.

Coalton social workers more or less agree that the parents that walk in with their eyes open constitute about half of all foster homes-in-training going through the licensing process. Afterward, the majority understand that, as in Sharon's example, love can take the form of due diligence without expectation of special moments. That may not feel like hearts and flowers to the giver but very well could to the wary recipient. Safety and security are the watchwords and the goals. A foster kid may not expect you to love her (or she may hope that you will), but she would like to believe that meals will be regular, the bed her own, any rules and chores clear and unchanging—things that even foster homes like the Cattle Farm provide.

If on top of that stability you show interest—"How was your day? Would you like to learn to play the flute? Have you ever driven a car before?"—a child may see that as friendship leading to trust leading to affection leading to love. Or she may feel invaded. Each child is unique, and each parent's motivation different. There are no magic formulas or assured methods. Foster parents who have done multiple placements for good reasons learn to hope that kids who have been betrayed most of their lives can recognize commitment when they see it. Social workers across Coalton affirm it is also a goal many parents reach, even in foster families the public would be quick to condemn.

Dale covers this tangled quagmire pretty well the day he joins Beth and me at the Riverside Bakery. I lay out my thoughts: if most of the parents want their children to love them, and the children want to feel safe, then isn't the whole thing about meeting the right families so true love will blossom? Is that why kids bounce through "good" homes so much, because the parents are looking for the right match?

Not really, says Dale. Think of it as more like an arranged marriage. "Nobody wants to say it's not about love, not at first. Good fosters might treat these children as a job to do, making conscious choices to ask how their day went, to remember they don't like onions, to sit down and do homework with them, all conscientious decisions rather than instinctive maternal or paternal love. That's not a bad home. That's a great home. Affection is born under stranger circumstances than determined commitment. Emotional involvement comes in many flavors, and that's what we're looking for in a great home."

In other words, familiarity breeds love. At least that's what the social workers are hoping for. The concept of a loving foster home is a moving target. Picture a horizontal line, suggests Cassie. At one end are excellent adoptions; at the other, abusive homes where kids are shouted at, told they're no good, perhaps hit, denied food, and so forth. According to Cody (and the other social workers, and Facebook pundits, and everyone else in America), there are about as many truly loving homes as there are pure evil ones; these are the smallest percentages on each end of the continuum. One in ten, say the regional insiders.

But then there's a big wavy line running down the middle of the continuum, dividing good homes from bad. Not all homes motivated by money are bad; not all altruistic homes are good. The good homes, in Beth's words, "buy the Pop-Tarts" because they care about the emotional and physical needs of the children they take on.

"The number one thing I'm looking for in a foster parent is compassion," Dale says. "Around here there are a lot of people who understand foster care needs because they've grown up raised by their grandparents. They'd starve themselves before they'd see a child go without food. We're looking for homes that will be focused on the kids. We don't care if they eat steak or baloney in that home, so long as they eat at a table where people are talking to them with kindness. Some things money can't buy."

Like recognizing that every day brings a new piece of a big puzzle, that some relationships take longer than others, that nothing and nobody is perfect, that the only true and final failure is abdicating responsibility, that small successes should be celebrated on the way to the larger goal. Those are the baseline attributes of an effective foster parent, says Dale.

"They aren't bought with money, and they're not necessarily enhanced by education. It all comes down to personal character. Do you give up easily? Are you a good listener, creative thinker, problem solver? Those are the people we need in this field, as parents and as workers. The rest we can teach you."

Cassie agrees with Dale's points when I repeat them for her, but she reiterates that this is an ideal rather than the reality in many foster homes. And that most foster kids aren't expecting emotional involvement either. If they receive it, they may wonder why. Trust is a slow build.

"You're in a home, multiple homes, where no one's rooting for you. By the time you're six or so, if you're used to not having someone root for you, you're not gonna fuss about it. Therein lies a big danger for society. We're gonna crash and burn under the weight of these kids who grow up unable to form attachments. They are the ones on track to become sociopaths because they can't feel their own emotional needs. No one was going to meet their needs, so they taught themselves to stop feeling them."

Emotional and societal needs in combination are what brought Margie and her husband, Sandy, to fostering. The couple live about an hour from their jobs in University City, she a professor in health sciences, he a lawyer. Their homestead lies outside Silton, a hamlet (population something less than a thousand) that includes one gas station, one pizzeria, one flower shop, and an Emergency Medical Services station.

"Too much buildup," Margie says with a wave of her hand. "I wanted to live outside Silton, not in it."

Fresh-faced with freckles, Margie has the kind of red hair and pale skin one associates with Ireland. Her hair held back by a headband, she exudes a no-nonsense air of command. After the birth of their third child, Margie had her tubes tied. The baby hadn't even turned one before the urge had come back, "so hard that I almost had the tubal reversed." A stay-at-home mom until her kids were all in school, Margie volunteered in his classroom when her youngest started kindergarten at Silton Elementary. (She was not yet teaching at the university.) There she began to see five-year-olds inadequately dressed, hungry, and coming to school unprepared emotionally or socially. The classroom was divided into achievement levels; her job was to take the group of children the teacher wasn't working with at any given time and read to them.

"But they wanted to talk, so we talked. And as they were talking about their lives, I realized, how selfish would that be, to have another baby when so many of these kids are out there, and they need so much support?"

At the same time, commercials for foster and adoptive parents were airing on the radio, and Margie heard them so often they haunted her. A child's voice would say, "I want a parent who . . ." and go on to describe various activities such as "reads to me" or "takes me to the beach." The tagline said that foster parents didn't need to be perfect, just available.

Having the means and the interest, the couple at first explored international adoption, even as the idea of a local one grew in Margie's mind. "I was brought back to reality by the kids that we have here in our schools and community. And by the massive price tag on international."

Next, Margie attended an agency's information session on therapeutic fostering, brought home some literature on the subject, and begged her husband to go to a subsequent open house with her. Resistant at first, Sandy cheered right up when he discovered that foster care under the state was not only free but paid for by the system.

"He said, 'It's fine with me so long as we don't have to spend $40,000 to get a kid internationally.' It was a bit of an eye-opener to both of us after me first getting my eyes opened at the school that you got a stipend for taking care of other people's children."

Which brings up money. Again.

"It never goes away," Cody says. "It has to be part of the discussion. Just not the focal point."

Although they have never met him, Margie and Sandy agree with Cody 100 percent. "It's the thing people don't ask us about, even at open-house days. They'll ask intimate things about family dynamics but not money. It's such a touchy subject. Not just in the adoption realm but in Silton and University City alike—and you couldn't find two places with more different economies. It's tacky to talk about money, culturally, but when you're talking about money and kids, it even feels gross."

When Margie first spoke with her husband about fostering, he thought it would wreck the family's finances, drain the college funds they'd planned for their first three children, slow down payment on the mortgage. When she showed him the payment system for therapeutic children, he sat down with a calculator and did the math. The family had no intention of using fostering to make money; they put the kids on their health policies at work and used Medicaid as backup. But they were also determined not to take on more than was sustainable over the long haul, which included college and career planning.

"I think that's something people are embarrassed to say, that they want to know if they can make it work financially. Why should we be? We're not in this for the money. There are a lot easier ways to make money, and who would play with children's lives like that? We crunched the numbers to make sure it would work."

When the family moved from fostering to adopting the three kids in their care, Margie and Sandy spoke at length with DSS and the private therapeutic agency about whether the payments would continue. This is a point many people don't seem to understand, that adoption doesn't necessarily stop the stipend for a foster child. The stipend depends on a needs assessment. Those wishing to see an example of one state's assessment system should do an Internet search for VEMAT (Virginia Enhanced Maintenance Assessment Tool). States vary.

"Nobody wants to talk about this, how it works, whether it's 'enough' of a stipend, how severe the children's special needs are. It does feel icky, the whole discussion about money, and yet it's a practical, logical part of 'Can we do it or not?' We're gonna bring these people in and do this within an existing family structure; it has to be fair and equitable between bio and adopted, a similar plan for the three coming in to how we look after our birth children; and you have to talk numbers in order to do that."

Margie and Sandy amortized the rate of savings they'd need in order to get their adopted children's college funds up to the level of their bio kids', given the number of years each had until college could be expected. They started taking that money out of the children's stipends each month and stashing it in bank accounts on their behalf. They watched the newbies until they felt they had some idea of extracurricular clubs they might want to join and paid fees or bought equipment if the child did. And they took them on vacations "where we got two hotel rooms instead of one because the stipend covered it."

She says it felt odd reckoning up the cash per child and how to use it, even though Margie believed in her own good intentions.[2] But the difference between those a little too concerned with funding and the conscientious number crunchers goes beyond how it might look on paper. Hearing about Margie and Sandy's mortgage and motel-room number crunching, Cody flicks his fingers in a dismissive gesture.

"It might've felt wrong to them, but that doesn't make it wrong. You know a good home when you see it. On paper they may look the same, but one visit, and you know. That's why we're supposed to do visits."

Margie thinks people sometimes do the assessments backward when taking on therapeutic children. "You have to realize as a foster family, 'OK, if we get that much, it's because we'll be welcoming a person who needs a lot of help.' Are we ready to do that, no matter what it costs? And we didn't just mean money. Emotionally. Time commitment. Fostering is really more 'Can the family dynamic and bio children and lifestyle you have now deal with chaos and kids coming in, and help them figure out who they are and all the other issues?' It's not about money, except to treat all the kids fairly."

But as much as she's seen people get hung up on money issues, Margie thinks there's another topic close to the heart of fostering that no one has asked her about.

"Nobody ever asks us about love. People dance around the question, 'Does it make a difference to you, the mom, whether your kid is bio or adopted?' Okay, yes, it does. There's this ethos that it shouldn't feel different, but it does. Maybe if we had adopted infants it wouldn't be different, but we didn't have time to meet our kids as babies, gaze into each other's eyes, and fall in love. People could misconstrue what they want to hear, I guess, but we don't love them equally; each one we love differently. They're unique individuals, and as you get to know them, you admire them, fall in love with them, and establish trust."

Margie gets annoyed with the idea that Cassie and others have espoused, that foster kids are often too damaged emotionally to bond, that they rarely reciprocate love and appreciation. "That whole pop psychology thing—'Can you really bond with foster kids?' Please. My nineteen-year-old doesn't bond, and that one came out of my body. He loves us, and we love him, but he's his own person, independent, self-contained. I have a bio kid who is less bonded than two of my younger ones. The baby of the family, Melody, came to us as a four-year-old little terror, and she was glommed to my legs for two years."

Each child has his or her own story, Margie concludes. They're all different, and it does make a difference that foster parents inherit mysteries without the background of enjoying those times "when they adore you and you adore them, just going in at night staring at their little faces sleeping in the crib. It takes longer, and it doesn't feel the same or happen the same way. It doesn't happen in a rush; it sneaks up on you as you get to know them, and one day you realize you've been in love, and maybe they are too.

"I feel as fiercely protective of them, as dedicated to helping them reach where they want to go, as my first three kids. I regret that we didn't get to protect them from the beginning. They're our responsibility, our joy, and our loves."

Hearing this quote from Margie later, Dale smiles. "That's what I'm talking about," he says. "That's a payback money can't buy."

8

Love, Understanding, and Fecal Matter

Nobody would believe this story, because nobody would believe I as a Catholic woman would do such a thing. But when I had foster kids, the oldest one was a developmentally delayed girl. When she was fifteen, I realized she had to be pregnant. Now I watched this girl and her brother like a hawk. I still think it was someone at her school. I had begged DSS to get her on birth control. Which they wouldn't pay for, so I did out of my own pocket. But she didn't take them or it failed or whatever, and her belly started getting round, her skin looked different, you know. We went to the doctor, and she confirmed it. Now I didn't have the authority to sign for an abortion. And then my church—don't go there. This girl couldn't raise a baby. I'm old. I'll be dead before that baby would have graduated high school. I took her out of state and paid for it myself. I'm pretty sure I have at least twenty friends who would drop me like a rotten potato if they knew, you know. And what I did was probably illegal. But I loved this girl, you know. I'm not gonna turn her life into a pro-life debate. Life had given her enough to deal with. Just make sure nobody knows who I am.

—foster mom

LACEY, A schoolteacher, and I sat in one of East Hill's quaint little coffee shops. East Hill has a thriving downtown based on shopping local and eating organic; it's a hippie haven a little more than an hour from Great Rock. Articulate and calm, Lacey described a childhood friend who came to live with her family because "her foster family were like starving her, literally. She went to live with my Aunt Annie because I begged her to take Serena in. She'd had foster kids before, she and my uncle. He died a few years ago."

It is the curse of a tight-knit region that people recognize one another easily. The more Lacey spoke of her aunt, the more I became convinced that she was a friend of mine from Great Rock. Finally, I asked outright, using a couple of identifiers rather than her name. Did Annie work in . . . ? Did she go to church at . . . ?

Lacey's eyes flew wide. "That's her! Wow, how weird you know her." She paused and laughed. "No, not weird. I've been in East Hill too long." (Many of East Hill's residents are not from the Coalfields.)

Annie and I had attended church cantatas together and lunched to-gether, and she'd been a regular at my bookstore's special events, yet she'd never mentioned being a foster parent. I sent her a Facebook message, sit-ting in my car after lunch with Lacey, and explained I'd been talking to her niece. Five minutes later, she replied that she'd meet me at the bookstore; she had heard about my research and wondered when I'd get around to her. Lacey had texted her I'd be calling.

"You might have mentioned you were a foster mom," I shot back.

"As much talking as you were doing around town, I knew you'd figure it out eventually." I could hear the smirk in her return text.

Hearing Annie's story of fostering felt less like an interview than like lunch with a friend. Annie and her husband, Howard, decided to become emergency foster parents when they discovered they couldn't have a bio-logical child. Howard was a mine supervisor, Annie a school nurse. She had seen foster kids and kids who should have been in foster care in her exam room for more than a decade and had reported many of them to DSS. For his part, Howard had watched miners struggling with injury succumb to prescription painkiller abuse, and the slide into chaos this brought their families. Extended-family adoptions, formal and informal, ran amok in the coal-mining culture. Substance abuse in Coalton was less about the dealing of drugs than about dealing with the pain that led to painkiller addiction.

The couple not only felt grounded in the issues but had specialty skills developed from their professions. Fed up with needy kids ignored by the system, Annie and Howard wanted to serve as examples to other adults of how important fostering is, while diverting children from destructive life paths.

Annie and Howard knew themselves to be open-hearted people, quick to attach. They didn't want an adoption option with every child they assisted, so they went for emergency fostering instead. Placements would be short, sudden, and urgent, loving but not lengthy. It felt like a good, logical decision. (That's how Margie and Sandy started, as well as Sam and Becky; it's a good way to ease into foster care and test one's mettle, social workers affirm.)

For Annie and Howard, it was more. "You know that saying, 'And God said HA!'?" Annie asks, a gleam of suppressed laughter in her eyes. "That pretty much covers how things went."

Almost as soon as they had their license, Annie became pregnant. Their daughter was a year old when the phone rang. The couple hadn't offered to foster since the pregnancy and had all but forgotten about their licensure, so it startled them to hear a disembodied voice from someone who said she worked with DSS, asking if they could take in a sixteen-year-old boy for two weeks.

"Seth was a sweet kid, gentle, just kind of fit in with us right away. He had a way with Lena [their daughter], and I don't think he was trying to be charming so he could stay; he honest-to-goodness liked kids. He could get her to laugh when no one else could. He turned into her protective big brother."

Two weeks stretched into a school year, and then Seth's birth mother asked him to come home for the summer. Drugs had not been involved in his removal from her home; she had put the kids in foster care after moving in with a man who didn't want children. The kids all returned home that June, but when school started she drove them back to the DSS office and dropped them off with their belongings.

"Bye, be good." Annie imitates the mother's wave and rolls her eyes, then chokes back a sudden sob.

Annie and Howard talked with Seth and his social worker, but by then the rising senior had enjoyed an entire summer of personal freedom, away from the curfew and chores imposed at his former foster parents' place. He decided that returning might be a mismatch and went instead to a group home run by a church; the home had a reputation for lax supervision. In

December, he called and without explanation asked if he could come back to Annie and Howard's. They made sure he understood their expectations and set a probation period. He passed with flying colors and stayed with them until his high school graduation. Although they offered to let him stay on at their expense (his stipend for foster care ended on his eighteenth birthday), Seth decided to move in with his uncle after graduating.

Seth kept in touch with his foster parents as life moved on. He married and had two children, divorced, and returned to Annie and Howard's house off and on when he needed a place to stay. He was in a custody battle with his former wife, and he sometimes brought the children to visit "Grandma Annie and Grandpa Howard" when he had them for the week. When their mom kicked her drug habit for good, she and Seth remarried and moved to a nearby city. The family now includes four children, and Seth works as a certified nursing assistant.

Seth's is a celebrated story in foster care circles because Annie and Howard supported their foster son emotionally and financially from the age of sixteen through twenty-six, including inviting him and his children to live with them on separate occasions during tough times. (Seth inherited clinical depression from his biological father.)

Annie and Howard took in a foster daughter during the time Seth moved to his uncle's. Gina was twelve when her mother died; she floated between relatives and developed drinking issues. An intelligent and popular girl, she stayed with Annie and Howard for eighteen months. The couple adored her and would have adopted her, but she didn't want to be adopted, for complex legal reasons. They offered instead to make her a permanent-placement foster, which is tantamount to adoption without taking the family's last name. Annie and Howard hoped this would afford her the stability to go to college while living at their place free of rent with meals provided. They helped her apply for scholarships and put the paperwork in for permanent guardianship.

It all looked like a done deal, until one day a legal document arrived. Without their knowledge, Gina had petitioned the family court to emancipate her so she could go live with her older sister. The court had granted Gina's request.

Annie and Howard felt lied to and upset, but the emancipation became the tip of the iceberg when they learned of the list of things she had alleged about activities at their house. It stopped just short of outright abuse.

"It was kind of her M.O. at that time, her survival technique. Gina was really smart; she'd been in the system since she was twelve, and she knew how to manipulate it. I don't think she'd ever really known somebody who loved her for who she was. She wanted to be emancipated so she could live with her sister, and she didn't care what it took to make that happen." Annie speaks calmly from a distance of ten years but adds with a wry smile, "Don't get the wrong idea. At the time I was inarticulate with rage."

Annie confronted Gina in a phone call, and Gina's response came down to, "Hey, do it to others before it's done to you." But Gina also called Annie from time to time over the next few months, "talking to me like a regular adult. She was still drinking, but she'd not gotten into drugs like her sister."

Gina left her sister's place to avoid getting sucked into the substance abuse that had claimed so many relatives. She moved in with a boyfriend, but he kicked her out without warning about a year later.

"My phone rang. She'd always loved us, always respected us, please could she come home? That kid." Annie closes her eyes and shakes her head with a faint smile.

Gina stayed six months the second time around, playing Barbies with seven-year-old Lena and taking her for McDonald's soft-serve cones every week, patiently waiting while Lena exhausted the play area's delights.

"Gina had a very particular set of problems. She'd seen trauma, been abducted at gunpoint. The last conversation she had with her birth mother, just before her mom OD'd, was her screaming at her mom that she hated her. She had baggage, and we trusted her with Lena. Her way of thanking us, I think, were those weekly walks."

Nothing ever went wrong, Annie adds. "Howard and I weren't stupid, and this is a small town. We knew what happened, whether she met any-body there, all that stuff. Gina played it safe with her little sister. If she hadn't, we wouldn't have trusted her."

Gina married a man with two daughters and moved to East Hill, that cheerful little town where I'd interviewed Lacey. The couple had two sons of their own. Gina and Annie have regular "mom talks," swapping stories, discussing their takes on parenting. Most Sunday nights, when the phone rings, it's Gina. And when Howard was diagnosed with late-stage cancer, Gina and her husband, Ted, came to visit, held his hand, and told him what a difference the couple had made in her life.

"They came three times while he was sick. The last was the weekend before he died. She feels like family. She'll always be our daughter. It didn't have a thing in the world to do with money. To be honest, there wasn't enough money in the world to make me deal with Gina if I hadn't loved her for who she was. She was a messed-up little whirlwind of too-smart-for-her-own-good. And she's my daughter."

After Gina, the quagmire of social-service craziness turned the couple's journey sour. They took in a medically fragile child, two-year-old Joy. Sadly enough for the stereotypes that abound about Coalton, her parents were cousins—and renowned for being meaner than rattlesnakes, higher than kites, and good shots with a rifle. They lived on top of Bald Knob, in a backwoods cabin and a couple of dead RV hulls pulled together to house the family.

Rather than remove the neglected children of this couple—who rarely sent their offspring to school and didn't keep follow-up doctor appointments after emergency-room visits for suspicious bone breaks—the caseworker tried family intervention planning. That did not go well, so the caseworker arranged for home-based nursing help instead, probably because she figured she'd never get those kids off Bald Knob.

A nurse went once a month to check on the tube-fed two-year-old and to see how the twin born with a congenital heart defect was progressing. The same person rarely went twice. About six months into this unsatisfactory arrangement, a young man named Rocky was the nurse of record. Six foot six and afraid of no man, Rocky entered this "cave of nastiness" to find the little girl with the feeding tube lying on a urine-soaked mattress, her butt stuck to it with fecal matter. Skin dirt-crusted, hair matted, she weighed fifteen pounds.

Intervention turned to rage. Against the parents' wishes but with little trouble from the dad so many feared, Rocky took Joy and her brothers in his car back down the mountain, and from the hospital, he called CPS.

"I believe the phrase is 'ripped them a new one,'" Annie says. When confronted, the caseworker said no one could get Joy and her siblings off the mountain because none of the neighbors would complain against the parents, and none of the nurses making visits had ever said anything about the conditions before. The father had an unproven reputation of molesting neighbors' children and apparently had threatened to harm the kids of anyone who "called the law" about how he raised his own.

Annie was asked to take in little Joy as an emergency foster because her nursing skills made her and Howard's home suited to medically fragile children. She tried over the next month to stabilize Joy, but the tiny girl developed pneumonia and started running a fever. Following a trip to the doctor, Joy wound up in an ambulance, riding to the children's hospital in University City. Annie sat next to her.

What happened next is one of those surreal stories that stop people from becoming foster parents and give social workers a bad rap. The doctors asked Annie to agree to certain stipulations about Joy's care. Annie told them, as she had been trained to do, that she was the emergency foster and didn't have the legal right to sign anything for the child. Joy's caseworker was called, and this is where things get really confusing.

DSS should have been the legal decision maker, but rumor had it the bio father could be a true charmer when needed. Annie had always felt, since Joy had come to her house, that one of the social workers was "soft" toward the father's "undefended" rights. It will never be clear if what happened next was the result of someone's genuine mistake or a deliberate misstep. For whatever reason, a deputy sheriff was sent up the mountain to tell the parents that their middle daughter was fighting for her life in the hospital. Not long after, he radioed back that Joy's father was in his patrol car, headed down the mountain.

From Annie's point of view, an enraged man was on his way to the hospital where she—the emergency foster parent who against this father's wishes had taken custody of his daughter— sat alone, without a car and no way to get home until her husband came to fetch her that night.

That's not how the father might have seen it, or how a sympathetic portrayal would show him. He might well have believed that he was coming to save his daughter's life because DSS was trying to kill her. (There had been discussion surrounding a do-not-resuscitate [DNR] order.) He was the dad; decisions were his; his daughter was in the hands of government bureaucrats who didn't care and would be thinking about money and their own agenda rather than her welfare.

Annie is having none of that.

"This was a child so dirty it took me a week to get her clean. I'd worked a month to get her stable on that tube. What kind of parent lets those things happen? What kind of man was he? And why in the hell did they tell him I was at the hospital?"

Annie appealed for help to Joy's caseworker, who apologized but offered no immediate assistance; she had to wait for the family and couldn't drive Annie home. ("I still think it was her supervisor [who got the bio father involved]," Annie pauses to mumble during our interview.)

Joy's story is a physical metaphor of the triangulated tension playing out again and again, usually with less drama or visible life-and-death decision-making. Parents are pitted against caregivers inside a system that pays social workers to choose one party but then judges them for that choice. It's a classic case of rights versus responsibilities; children are shuffled toward what looks like safety but might not be, only to be yanked back by the bonds of family, strengthened by legal ties.

Should there have been a DNR? Who had the moral right to decide Joy's care, even if DSS had the legal one? In this case, one would expect that no person who knew Annie or the father would have had difficulty choosing a "righteous" side—and yet at least one social worker probably did. This triangle between the family, the system, and the fosters never goes away. How often can a child stand to be the focus of three disputing factions?

The situation didn't go away so much as get defused for Annie and Howard. For the second time, Rocky saved the day. He was on shift in the hospital, heard the little girl he'd driven down the mountain had come in, dropped by to see her, and learned from Annie (whom he knew professionally) what was going on. The nurse called his shift manager and said he was taking Annie to dinner; the manager should call once Dad had gone. Howard came to collect Annie as soon as he could, and the couple thought the drama had ended.

Nope. The next week, when Joy had been stabilized, her father or DSS having refused to sign the DNR, the little girl went back to Annie and Howard's. Not three days later, Annie fielded a call from yet another member of the DSS team working on Joy's case. A family services case manager had assisted the father in petitioning for visitation rights with his daughter. Family court had granted his request. Since it was medically inadvisable for Joy to travel, the visitation would have to be in her foster home.

Annie and Howard's house. Where they lived with their nine-year-old daughter.

"I left the gentleman in no doubt as to the possibility of that happening," Annie says with a smile. "My response may have involved profanity." Annie still bristles at a certain tone in that social worker's approach. "I think the father must have spun that same old sob story: children ripped from loving arms, et cetera. He was all about the father's rights being violated. I remember screaming, 'Did you see Joy when she was at the hospital?'"

Annie feared the father already knew where she lived. She had heard stories from other foster parents about caseworkers leaving documents on their desk, either by carelessness or complicit sympathy, so that parents would see the names and addresses of their children's foster parents. Such laxity has disappeared, Cody would like people to know. A caseworker who "pulled this stunt" under his watch would be fired.

As it turns out, Joy's bio father didn't know where Joy lived and never found out. Someone—probably an ad litem, perhaps a more senior supervisor like Dale—stepped in and restored a little common sense to the equation. Still, Annie gets angry all over again when she recalls hearing that "supercilious" voice tell her that visitation had been granted with no input from her. In retrospect, that was the moment when she and Howard reassessed how worthwhile what they were doing could really be.

"We believed in commitment, faithfulness, seeing the task through." Annie throws her hands in the air. "We had pledged stability to every child who passed through our home. But this felt like a threat we couldn't have, not around Lena and not for ourselves."

They told Joy's new caseworker she would have to be moved. "She tried a guilt trip on me, which didn't work. It felt like a betrayal on their part," Annie says, clenching the sides of her chair and using a sing-song voice: "'He's done this, he's done that, we're too scared to do anything about him, and oh by the way he's gonna come over and you have to let him in.'"

It took some heart-hardening on both their parts, but the couple stopped responding to requests to provide emergency care. "It was a threat we could not have."

Still, Annie and Howard reentered foster care a few years later through a backdoor when their niece Lacey, then a junior in high school, mentioned a friend with miserable circumstances in a difficult foster home. Serena had to buy her own meals. To do this, she had a job at the same fast-food restaurant as Lacey but was often late or missed work because the family refused to let her use their car. When she didn't work . . .

"When that child came to stay with us, I swear she ate for three days straight."

The couple sighed as Lacey begged them to help her friend, then did so, at first privately, then through DSS so that they could use the stipend to help her buy a car. They taught Serena how the monthly payments would work, how to write a check from the account, how long the money would be available, and so on. Serena was an excellent student they knew could get scholarships, so they helped her fill out applications. They also suggested she go to college locally so that she could save money by continuing to live with them. It was all going so well, and then "she met this guy."

The guy was known in town; he had dated another coworker of Lacey and Serena's, and he had been abusive to her. Howard laid down the law; Serena could not bring him to their house. There was Lena to consider. He also told her what she did outside those boundaries was her choice, but in his opinion she was making a dumb one if she continued to see this loser.

Serena took that "about as well as any teenager would" and moved in with the abusive boyfriend. He beat the car they'd helped her buy into scrap metal with a baseball bat. He destroyed her cell phone. He may or may not have broken her arm. His family was in a position to set him up with a business; Serena severed contact with Annie and Howard and took over running her husband's firm on behalf of the family. The couple had children. There were no pictures or Christmas cards to Annie and Howard.

Once, as Annie crossed the parking lot of Great Rock's grocery store, she heard a voice call to her. Serena sat in a car, waiting for her daughter to finish dance class at a nearby studio.

"She just started right in: 'I want you to know that I will always appreciate what you two did for me, and think of you as my mother, but my husband doesn't want me to have anything to do with you. He doesn't let me talk about my upbringing. The kids don't know I grew up in foster care. So I won't see you anymore, but thank you.'"

Annie says that moment made something clear to her. "It was all very stressful, but Howard and I were—and I still am—the kind of people who wanted to make an impact on somebody else's life, leave them better than we found them. Going through all these times, it seemed very frustrating, and we got angry and kept thinking we're not gonna do this anymore; but now, looking back at it, you can see long-term the effects on those kids.

Those teenagers we got 'too late in life to make a difference.' No, we did make a difference."

Annie has little patience with social workers who complain about foster parents being in it for the money without caring. "I think often they saw us and the other conscientious ones as annoying. We couldn't really talk to most of them about the problems our foster kids were having. Take Gina: all that guilt about her mom turned into drinking, but they didn't want to do anything about it. They said, 'Oh, we have no resources, maybe we can get her into counseling.' They just wanted somebody, in my opinion, that didn't rock the boat. Their actions, to me, said, 'Take these kids just for the money and be quiet, don't complain about how little we see them, don't say this is what the child needs.' They didn't want us to be proactive or advocate for the children we had. Like when Gina moved out into an emancipated apartment but was living with her boyfriend, which was against the rules, and I'd tell them he's living there, and they didn't care."

The line between "we're so hard pressed and the needs are so great, we're too busy to check your concern" and "we're so hard pressed and the needs are so great, we don't give a flip" looks suspicious to Annie. She moved back to school nursing after Joy left their home, and frustration coursed through her veins once more as she and colleagues called DSS again and again about the same children. School teachers are required reporters, bound by law to let CPS know about any evidence of abuse or neglect such as bruises, malnutrition, excess dirt, and untreated medical conditions.

"The teachers and I would call, and threaten, and document. And from our point of view, the parents practically had to kill a child to get him or her out of their home. I'm all for family cohesion, but it just got ridiculous."

Reacting to her story, Cody couldn't help himself when I sided with Annie. The words burst like a dynamite blast through rock as he waved his hands in frustration. "I guarantee you they *were* trying, but when's anybody gonna realize there aren't enough safe places for kids 'round here? Everybody's frustrated. Everybody's trying. Ain't no fairy godmother gonna fix this."

Annie might have been the closest thing to a fairy godmother—if an annoying one—DSS thought they would ever see. They used her as one soon enough. She'd been keeping a close eye on one particular family from her school that several teachers thought might be in crisis. Dana lived with her sister, birth father, stepmother, and half sister atop a mountain with no roads to speak of, in a place similar to (but in a different school district from) Bald Knob. No running water, and reports of inadequate food. The two youngest girls volunteered to their teacher that Mom and Dad had been in a fight so big they were afraid they would kill each other, and one of them had spanked the youngest girl when she tried to intervene. The difference between "spanked" and "hit" is not a conversation Annie cares to have; the youngest girl had bruises, and the school duly reported these injuries to DSS. The teachers were told that abuse had been alleged previously but that no one had been on a home visit to check yet. In addition to calls about other children, Annie and her fellow teachers kept phoning every time they observed one of these sisters dirty, bruised, or too hungry to have been eating at home.

"And a few weeks after we started this harassment campaign, which is what we called it, we got a call back. They'd gone out and checked on the food and running water. Unfounded. Everything was fine."

But the oldest girl told staff members that she feared for her and her siblings' lives, so Annie took her aside. It was March, the weather cool but getting warmer. She told Dana, "The next time there's a big fight you take your sisters with you and go to a neighbor, even if you have to walk a long way. Then get them to call the police." About a week later, Dana did, and they headed down the mountain road after dark, one girl barefoot.

At that point, CPS took the girls from the home. And their social worker came to see Annie at the school and said they had no place to put the girls, together or separately, so could she please keep them, and thanks so much.

"It almost felt like punishment," Annie says. "'You wanna be a hero, lady? Fine. You take them.'"

Howard and Annie took them. And they soon discovered that the learning disabilities displayed by two of the girls paled in comparison to the social issues all three exhibited.

"I couldn't even take Dana to Walmart without her being in some man's face she didn't know. She was all over guys of all ages—inappropriate hugging, flirting. I would turn my back, and she'd be gone. I sat her down and talked to her: 'Honey, you can't do this, it's not safe; it's not right.' She was sixteen at the time."

Despite an attraction to men that suggested childhood sexual abuse and seemed to have no boundaries, Dana never tried anything with Howard. As Annie put it, Howard had "boundaries strong enough for everybody."

The sisters were also swift to anger and prone to striking one another, emulating the way they'd seen conflict resolved at home. Annie and Howard tried to teach them other methods of conflict resolution alongside basic household cleanliness. They were assigned chores: washing clothes, cooking, cleaning. The girls complained to their social worker that Howard and Annie made them work too hard. This particular accusation made their foster mom snort with laughter because everything took a lot longer when the girls were involved, and the house hadn't been clean since they'd arrived.

"That was the point. They needed to have some basic skills because they were way late in life to be trying to build them. And instead of support, I got investigated. They couldn't go up the mountain to find out if there was food in the house, but they come talk to me about 'slave labor'?" Annie sighs. "But it's common for foster kids to do that. They've never had structure and discipline—in other words, chores—before."

Herein lies one of the great dilemmas of the foster care system. Annie and Howard did what the Cattle Farm Boss did: told the girls they had to work if they wanted to stay in their home. They say it was because they wanted the girls to learn to do tasks their parents had never taught them. Which is the same justification the Boss gives: canning, cooking, and cleaning are important skills. Anyone who meets Annie would understand her intrinsic integrity, her sense of cautious optimism about making positive impacts, her reasoned approach to realistic intervention. No one would categorize her as the same kind of foster mom as the Boss; and as a home visit revealed to Cody, there was a considerable difference between what the Boss described as happening in her weekly reports and what her foster children said they experienced. But on paper Annie and the Boss could look the same. And on paper, Joy's father could come across as a sympathetic person.

The difference is easy to discern, says Cassie, dismissing this speculation as "hairsplitting." Annie and her husband were emotionally invested in their foster children. How does one document "emotional involvement"? The foster care system's policy makers say to use home visits and regular reviews of the family's reports, plus to document all interactions with the child. The workers on the ground say, "HA!" If they had time to read and follow up on the paperwork alone from an average of thirty cases per worker, at half an hour per child that's fifteen hours from a forty-hour workweek—both to read parental reports and to write theirs.

Besides—and here we return to an observation social workers are loath to engage with—distinguishing between Annie and the Cattle Farm Boss isn't a judgment call most people in the foster care world appear interested in making. Good and good enough can look an awful lot alike in a system with too few homes and too many critics. Annie sees the irony as well. At first, she tried to draw a support system of other foster parents around her, but when she realized that many of them were in it for the stipend, she stopped attending meetings.

She also recognizes that how she handled the sisters differed from her previous and following fosters: strict, swift, and less carefully considered than working to a list.

"It was almost like desperation. They were so old to be learning these really simple things, and I felt a kind of panic to instill these basic skills in them. Fueled by guilt, too, I guess, because I told their caseworker, as soon as the school year was over, I wanted them out of my house. Dana was going to get pregnant; it was inevitable, her so unable to think through decisions and so up in men's faces."

Along with the basics of cooking, which the girls liked, and cleaning, which they didn't, she taught them about condoms, sanitary pads, basic first aid, simple self-defense, and "how to say no." Also about choices once they were pregnant. And she nagged their caseworker: get all three of them birth control, and get it now.

That didn't happen. Once school was out, Annie kept her promise to send the girls back to DSS—a decision she still somewhat regrets. The weekend after they went to a new foster, Dana ran away to a party, went home with a man she met there, and came back pregnant.

"What part of 'get her on birth control' was unclear?" Annie wonders. "It's not even like it costs that much." After an abortion, Dana got pregnant again, when her newest foster mother let her boyfriend come home and spend the weekends with her.

"I'm gonna say that was a paycheck family." Annie's voice holds something between sadness and sarcasm. "Or maybe she was just a hopeless romantic. Anyway, she let the boyfriend stay, which is against the rules, and then sent Dana back to DSS when she was six months pregnant. Pardon me while I roll my eyes."

Dana got emancipated and went to live with her boyfriend's parents, paying rent from her new job now that she'd left school (without a diploma). When the baby was six weeks old, the boyfriend's parents kicked her out and kept their grandson; Dana did not protest. It is unclear whether she understood that she could protest losing her son, until her caseworker asked if that's what Dana wanted. She said no, so DSS helped her go to court to petition for her rights. Annie did not get involved in that action.

But she was about to get involved in a big way again, and pretty much against her and Howard's will. Right after Dana's petition for custody was granted, DSS called Annie and Howard. The couple had a trailer at the back of their property. The same social worker who had cajoled her into taking the girls the first time asked Annie to let Dana and the baby live there.

"You're crazy!" Annie shouted. "No!"

The social worker wasn't finished. She contacted the resource teacher assigned to work with pregnant girls in the county school, a good friend of Annie's. The resource teacher laid it out for Annie over a friendly lunch—"ambush," Annie snorts. Dana had nowhere to go and no one on her side, and she didn't want to give her son to his father's parents. Which was the next move if she didn't get help, because DSS had helped her promise the judge she would have a safe place to live right away.

Dana moved into the trailer in September. The caveat was that a relative of Howard was coming to stay the following June while he attended summer courses at the nearby college, so her arrival stipulated at its inception a deadline for leaving.

"That might be what saved my sanity," Annie says now. "By then my mom was in home care for Alzheimer's, and I was traveling every day after work to look after her."

Annie laid down a few rules: the boyfriend could not spend the night in the trailer, which had to be kept clean. Dana would return to school. Annie went in several times during the first six weeks and helped Dana clean, but this turned into Annie's cleaning while Dana chatted with her boyfriend. Annoyed, Annie announced she was done helping with the cleaning, although she continued to pick mother and son up in the mornings, dropping Dana at school and the baby at day care. After a few visits, she began to smell cat pee. Dana's family-preservation worker had found a cat, which Dana decided she wanted.

"I didn't have the strength to fight it," Annie says with a sigh. "I thought I was picking my battles. Really, I was just tired."

When the baby was sick at day care, Annie would take the day off work to get him seen by a doctor or taken to the hospital. Some nights she wound up driving the boyfriend home herself because he had no transportation, which really annoyed her. "It was open manipulation: let me spend the night. No."

Annie pushed the girl's support team to move up her departure. They finally got her a HUD apartment in a nearby housing complex. Annie went to help her move and found the extra bedroom in the trailer full of dry cat feces. She lost control.

"I told her, 'I hope you do lose your baby; you don't deserve this child. I've done everything I can for you, and you still choose to live like this. Why? You've had everyone bend over backward to help you; why act like this?'"

Dana waited until Annie was done yelling, then said she wanted Howard to drive her because she didn't want to see Annie ever again. Howard drove in silence to the housing development, Dana in the backseat surrounded by boxes and bags of her stuff. Meanwhile, Annie found Dana had left several items of clothing and other belongings in the trailer. These she packed into a box. She included with them every dried cat feces she could find.

"The only thing I kept was the cat. It wasn't her fault, the cat's. Dana called later and wanted the cat. I got it fixed and took it to her."

Despite the assistance, at the housing complex Dana wound up getting into a fight that resulted in charges, and her boyfriend's parents won custody of the grandchild. Dana married a navy man and moved East. She regained custody of her baby and still posts Facebook pictures of the little boy, now in elementary school.

"He looks good," Annie says. "I think she's gotten her act together and become a decent mom." Dana also sends messages to Annie via Facebook, like one that arrived just the week before our interview: "I still see you as a mother figure, and Howard was the only father I've ever known."

Annie remains cautious. "It's still a little strained between us."

Right after Dana left, Annie's mother passed. Soon after came Howard's sudden cancer diagnosis, and Annie left her job to look after him. After Howard's death, she went back to school nursing.

"Social Services listens to me more now. I tell them that I want to hear back from them what the findings are when we report a child from school and give them two or three weeks to get back to me. And if they don't I go higher. I have become what they call a professional pain in the butt."

And a Community Service Board[1] member, working with child protection related to substance abuse in Great Rock and beyond. From her new position she has been able to address many of the issues she saw from the other side of the table, and she feels this is where her contributions now lie. She has not returned to fostering. Partly, it's feeling that without her husband, it would be too daunting. "If you care, it hurts to foster. I wouldn't have emotional support like we gave each other before."

And partly, she doesn't want to deal with the fingerprinting, the financial disclosure, the invasive personal questions and home visits and constant scrutiny. "Even with nothing to hide, it's nerve-wracking. I'm too old to start over."

Still, she misses investing in the lives of teenagers.

"That's why I've applied to host an exchange student," she says with a wicked grin. "All the fun, half the responsibility, and they're better conversationalists."

9

Aging Out

My adoption was like a miracle. I'd been in this foster home before, and my parents had wanted to adopt me, but I got sent back to my birth mother. When she messed up again, they had kids in, boys, so there wasn't any place for me to be there.

I went to another foster home, but they [the first one] kinda kept track of me, and when they'd adopted the boys, they made their room bigger so they could share it, and adopted me. I didn't move in until I was sixteen, and it took us about six months to fast track the paperwork. My mom was just amazing. She wouldn't leave any of them alone. She was on a mission.

And they're not wealthy people, so they told me when I got there, we're going to help you apply for everything going to get financial aid to college because we can't pay for it. And they did. When I graduated from high school—that's not something every foster kid does—when I graduated, my mom and dad gave me a card. Inside they'd written, "Not many people know your story, and we know you don't like to tell it. Everything that's happened to you, you've turned into strength. Some kids fall under the weight of what happens to them in foster care, and some kids fly. You're our little bird soaring into life with your new wings, and we're so proud of you."

Then I'm already crying, right, and then they gave me a kitten. And it was like two presents. I'd always wanted a cat, but how was that possible

*growing up in the system? So now this cat, this gorgeous calico with a
personality that won't quit, she was mine.*

  *But it was also saying, "This is your home; this is where you live; go
or stay, we'll be here, looking after your cat. This is your home forever."*

—*adopted teen*

ANNIE'S EXPERIENCES were for the most part with teenagers, those with
just a couple of years left before they turned into adults in the eyes of the
state and the assistance stopped. It is the "danger zone," as some social
workers describe it, the liminal stage when a child has to turn into an adult,
whether he's been equipped to or not.

"These kids don't have a safety net," says retired social worker Karen,
her face grim. "Fall or fly, for real." (Karen was familiar with the adopted
teen whose letter is featured above.)

Karen is the adoptive mother of five special-needs children and was the
voice of wisdom for three generations of colleagues. She describes her career as avoiding promotion to administration for forty-five years so that she
could stay in the field and handle cases until the day she turned sixty-five.

"Honey, it ain't hard to avoid promotions when you're a woman working for the government." She winks.

The resident expert on what it means to age out in Coalton, Karen has
seen it done under four federal government administrations. Every social
worker for three counties around has her home number on speed dial.

"Aging out" is what it sounds like: a child who has not been adopted turns
eighteen and leaves the foster care system—be that from a foster family, a
permanent placement, a group home, or an emancipated-living situation.
Some foster kids get emancipated when they turn sixteen, depending on
circumstances. It is not always in their best interests for this to happen, as
emancipation comes with a temporary apartment and an expectation that
you will begin to pay back quickly. It does not come with college funding,
which is available if you age out of a foster family and apply.

Aging out is meant to happen only to foster kids, not those adopted. If
all goes according to plan, adopted children remain with their families once
they turn eighteen, just as biological children expect to do until they can

launch out on their own. According to Susan, the student ambassador for the college-retention program Great Expectations, about one in ten children aging out of Coalton's foster care system will start college. Perhaps one in ten of those will graduate.[1] Retention programs specific to foster students exist in most public colleges and universities.[2] Take Great Rock Great Expectations as an example. An educational psychologist runs it at a community college of 1,500 students. The support staff includes Susan as a student ambassador; the program hires former foster children for this position.

Great Expectations works to ensure each college student from a foster family receives the "only if you're going to school" monthly stipend (not usually available to emancipated kids). The organization also helps students apply for free housing via HUD and a tuition waiver. Electronic Benefits Transfer (EBT) payments while students are in college give them $2,400 up front with which to purchase a car and will assist with repairs as needed. Since many foster kids are unaware of this program, Susan makes sure they hear about it as soon as possible.

If all that sounds generous, people outside the community college's region need to visualize the area: few buses, no taxis, and who can safely ride a bike twenty-six miles to school on such winding mountain roads? The road from East River to Great Rock alone clings to the sides of mountains in ways city dwellers can't imagine. A car is not an optional piece of the puzzle for attending college or holding down a job in Coalfields Appalachia.

The Great Expectations director is an unapologetic advocate for college assistance when it comes to foster kids.

"It's a sweet deal. People complain sometimes that their tax dollars are going to support social programs, but you know what? I don't think anyone is owed anything in this life, yet I have a biased opinion when it comes to foster kids. Everything's been stacked against them for so long, they deserve something to help them get on their feet. And once they get there, they're gonna get off the state books. You want to help now or support them for the next fifty years because they can't get a job because they didn't go to college?"

These college students in return are required to maintain a passing grade point average and otherwise uphold the codes of conduct stipulated by the school: attend classes, don't break the "where to smoke and where to hang out" rules, and so forth. Unfortunately, this generosity can be problematic for newly minted adult foster children because it seems a little overwhelming.

Susan explains. "No one's ever taught us to balance a checkbook, set a budget, or generally understand the value of money, except that we never had any. We were going from a foster home where we barely got fed to one with an X-Box in our bedroom. We had no control over any of it. That doesn't teach you to manage money or appreciate what you've got. It'll get yanked off you tomorrow. That's what we learned coming through the system.

"Then we land in this apartment with that $664 a month stipend and a car we don't have to maintain, and the only bill we get is for the phone. It's not a lot of money, but it's enough to make someone go crazy. Some of the kids literally don't know how to do it. Plus, we're trying to go to college, so there's not a lot of time to concentrate on anything else. Odds are good, unless we landed in a good family, no one ever prepped us for this time in life."

Instead, students do the best they can until they turn twenty-one, when the payments stop. Cold. One month after your birthday, your apartment is gone and the checks don't come any more, and even if you're not finished with college, you'll have to figure out where to live and how to pay for it.

The director adds, "The government doesn't have exemptions for special circumstances, but some organizations in the community have given us funds. Last year we needed to assist someone who had to get her appendix out and missed a semester. There's no exception for something like that."

Susan bounced through foster care for ten years before being adopted by a family that couldn't afford to cover her college tuition. They helped her apply for financial aid.

"I was a little older than most kids when I got adopted, and they sat me down and said, 'Here's what we're putting aside for you, but it's not gonna cover much more than your books. We'll help you apply for a Pell Grant.' None of us knew then about Great Expectations, but that's how I got tuition. My parents love me, and they didn't, like, take the supplement they got for me and use it to buy a boat or anything. They just couldn't afford to send me to college, and they were very straight up about that when we were going through the adoption process. I live in my adopted home now, and I'll probably live there until I graduate college."

Susan has no patience with people who blame the kids coming out of foster care as "adults" for their circumstances when they turn twenty-one and have no prospects. Some might suggest that a foster kid is just like any other child: get a job and save up if you want to go to college, and budget your time right without goofing off so you finish on time.

"Do you know any twenty-one-year-olds around here who grew up in a 'normal' home, who had enough finances and determination to save the total cost of college tuition from the time she starts working, without a scholarship? Let alone one who's been trying to survive six new foster parents in a year. Oh yeah, we're so focused and prepared for these decisions."

However, there's a government plan for this situation, Susan adds, her voice taking on an edge. Semiannually, DSS holds a six-hour class to teach foster kids basic life skills. Basic banking skills (opening an account, checkbook maintenance, loan applications). Basic work etiquette (interview skills, appropriate clothing). Basic bill paying (how to interpret a bill, how to assess utility costs and set up a budget, online payments). About eighty kids attend these marathon sessions, which are held in central locations across multiple regions.

"You can see the students falling out as the day wears on. Some kids need more time. They don't grasp math quickly. And the guy up front is just clicking through his slides. But students who don't attend one of these sessions don't get a monthly support check. They go to this seminar and come home frustrated and confused, and we wind up delivering this info one-on-one, later, for those who really understand they need it. That's where they really get help. If they'll ask."

Most foster kids who start college don't finish. What happens to the ones who don't graduate, and to those who don't enter college in the first place? Don't expect to remain in the adoptive or foster home, say the social workers. They estimated that a little under 5 percent of the adopted kids and more than 90 percent of the fostered ones in Coalton will be asked to leave home when they turn eighteen.

Many people's images of what happens to aging foster kids are colored by *The Blind Side*, the inspiring movie in which Sandra Bullock portrays the adopting mother of Michael Oher. The family adopts him at the age of seventeen, and he turns into a football star. Social workers have a love-hate relationship with this film.

Cody's eyes roll toward the fluorescent lights. "What this triumph-of-the-human-spirit movie doesn't tell you is how much they would have spent feeding that young man. He was a football player. He was huge. He would've eaten like a horse. They could afford it. The rest of humanity isn't gonna keep a kid once his stipend stops."

What Cody is referencing in an offhand way is that families who adopt therapeutic foster kids lose the stipend for their care when the kids turn eighteen. Depending on the severity of the needs, the child may be eligible for other social assistance. The true story of Michael Oher's adoption happened less than two hours' drive from Cody's agency, but it's not one his team identifies with. Nor do they find all that many people like Annie, willing to help their teenaged responsibilities buy a car with the stipend money. Although they long to. More often, they find that the couples who have long-term fostered, or in some cases adopted a child "for life," go a little crazy when the payments stop.[3]

"The good ones are startled at themselves," says Beth. "I've seen parents who maybe meant it when they said, 'I love you now and forever,' who didn't realize how much it was going to affect them when the kid turned eighteen. Parents here don't tend to be wealthy. They haven't planned for this, the ones who are just trying to scrape by. Although some of the ones who were in it for the money the whole time, now they've been planning quite a while. They've already told their child she needs to have someplace to go within a week, a month, sometimes the day after their birthday. Long before they bring it up with us."

Some parents intend to plan ahead, as Sandy and Margie did in reality, but life and time slip past until suddenly they're confronted with a grown child whose stipend ends at the moment his needs become more complicated. And more expensive.

"No matter how much they thought they were, I saw maybe one in five parents prepared for their kids' aging out," says Karen. "The ones who got their kids very young and had truly bonded—you don't worry about them. But you see a house filling with permanent-placement teens, and you know what's coming. But listen, it's way too easy to judge them for it. Say they've been looking after a kid with developmental delays. He's all grown up now, weighs 325 pounds, and they're trying to feed him on their own—no more services—that's tough. They can say they love that man-child forever and ever, but love sometimes gets measured in money. Which is a terrible thing to say, but in adoptions overseas, parents weigh up their resources and choose to give their kids away. We call that love, and that's also love measured in money, and those parents are doing a good thing. Just saying."

What happens when that boy with mental disabilities hits eighteen? Nothing. Literally, nothing. He won't receive a diploma, and the vocational-training classes his stipend included are at an end. Everything his good conscientious parents have been receiving funds to give him stops cold. Does he have enough vocational training to bring income to the house and cover his food? Is he going to stay with them until they die?

Cody has a few things to say on this point. "This kid ain't gonna play football for Ol' Miss. He'll need help to live independently, never mind college. You wanna believe you can do the best for someone—you want the best for them, really believe you do—then suddenly the money's gone. Can you imagine the complicated tangle that becomes? I've watched good people deal with it. But it's so easy for the rest of the world to sit in judgment: 'How could you do that? How could you turn a poor needy child out of your home when you've been their support?' Please notice once again those critics aren't fostering."

Though she can be soft-spoken and has a matronly appearance, with her gray bun and sweater set, Karen's words sound as if they're falling from a razor blade, so sharply does she bite them off.

"At least most of those people who fail at the end have been trying. And the better ones are so startled by themselves, by what they feel when all the veils are lifted and all the help is gone. It's cyclical. The new parents are all gung ho; the old ones are jaded. Those new parents sit and cry in our offices, 'I just love these kids, I'll do whatever I can for them, even if I'm not getting paid'; and then they get within sight of twenty-one—actually, eighteen now; the law changed last year—and then all hell breaks loose, and they list a string of things that have been going wrong, justifying why they can't really be this boy's parents any more. It's reached the point where we [social workers] are just waiting for the inevitable."

When Karen says parents sit crying in social workers' offices, she means crying as they ask for the child to be removed from their home before she turns eighteen, so that the foster home doesn't look as though they threw her out on her birthday. Or wind up carrying any legal responsibilities going forward. "We get to be the bad guys. They start saying to us, 'We haven't been telling you what's going on, but it's gotten bad.' It's bad enough to deal with that for permanent fosters, but it's truly horrible when it's an adopted child."

Social workers work to prepare the kids once the first hint drops from parents, perhaps six months out from an upcoming birthday. Plans for thirty-, sixty-, and ninety-day progress in getting a job and moving out are put in place for all nonpermanent foster kids, but also when parents say words like "unexpected difficulties" or "emancipation as a better option" or "We're not gonna drop him like a hot potato, but he's getting to the age where . . ."

"Yes, they are. They're gonna move on to some other kid, and it will be a twelve-year-old. Now they can keep getting a paycheck for six more years. We see it very clearly for what it is. They say the kid goes, we have to help the kid go. And don't think the kid doesn't know. He does. She does. Your last rejection in the foster system is just before you hit the streets on your own. Great start. Or great ending to a series of rejections, starting with your birth mom. These kids can't catch a break." Beth sighs as she states her mind. She looks as though she's held this conversation before.

The rules for children aging out of regular or therapeutic foster care have changed several times in the last twenty years. Until recently, state funding existed[4] to taper therapeutic foster services off from the ages of eighteen through twenty-one. "One month it was there, the next it was gone, cut from the governor's budget. We heard it went to pay for road signs on highways. They needed it to post mileages." Barbie shakes her head in disgust, her blond ponytail swinging in outrage behind her.

Cody thinks the government should market a line of greeting cards for foster kids. "'Congratulations on turning eighteen; now get out there and pay us back in taxes.' Which is a sick joke. We didn't even have a month's warning this change was gonna happen. We got twelve kids in this situation this year alone. They're not college bound. What am I gonna do for them now?" Cody gives a deep sigh of frustration.

Kids have few options if they don't head for college and don't have homes willing to keep them. Many stay with friends and couch surf. The social workers are pretty cynical about their prospects, saying most will be on drugs within the year, unless they've got great friends with understanding parents. One in five will get picked up for minor theft or drug offenses or prostitution. Cody sighs as he delivers this statistic.[5]

"People think foster kids are criminals in training. They're not.[6] They're a thousand times more likely to be the victims. They've been vulnerable their whole lives. They're easy marks for pimps and pushers and scammers. And think about it: being from here, they're wanting to get to the big city, and they're gonna get swallowed up whole. Sitting ducks."

The bulk of these kids will look for their bio parents. They may already know where they are; Facebook is the bane of privacy for everyone these days, and many a child has friended a parent in secret. The story of "Lucy" is legend across Coalton. In fact, I heard it from so many people I thought the episode apocryphal at first.

Lucy was in high school, and although she knew she was adopted, she'd never met her birth mother. This missing connection became the subject of numerous essays Lucy wrote for English class. Lucy's bio mother called the school one day and asked to speak to Lucy, who was excused from class to use the office phone. How did her mother know where Lucy was? Lucy's adoption was via KinCare, in-family, and her bio mom knew it was just a matter of time until she found out which school she was in.

"You tell people not to post pictures [on Facebook and other social media] of the kids and stuff, at least not before they're adopted, but it doesn't matter. There's no such thing as privacy in a small town, and there's no such thing as privacy online. Between the two, secrets don't get kept." Karen makes a dismissive gesture, as though flicking cigarette ash.

When her birth mother asked Lucy if she wanted to meet, the teacher told her she could go during class later that week. Lucy drove from Troutdale High down to the mall in Tri-Cities and met her mother at the food court. All without permission from or the knowledge of her adoptive parents, and with the complicity of the schoolteacher.[7]

Lucy's mother was delighted to see her daughter, promptly asking to borrow money. These funds Lucy, in turn, tried to borrow from her extended family. That's how they found out about the contact, and they went ballistic. Get used to it, say social workers. Parents will track their kids one way or another (most commonly through extended family and social media) and ask for many things. Among the most common requests, say the kids, are information on the whereabouts of other family members, pills from the child's or a family member's prescriptions, and money.

Beth shows a rare moment of frustration with one of her former cases. "You've been listening to this kid for the past five years say, 'I hate my mom. She chose drugs over us. I hate her.' And the day she turns eighteen, she hitchhikes to Louisiana to find her."

These family track-downs rarely go well, but Cody clings to one story when it did.

"Two years ago, I had a kid go do that, but one day maybe three months later out of the blue she turned up on the steps outside, fifteen minutes before closing." He gestures out the window of his office building. "She doesn't say hello, doesn't say anything about how she got back, she just says, 'Help me. I can't live like her.' We bent every rule in the book to get her a safe place to live. She started working at a call center. Got married. She's working on her nursing degree now at the college. On the bad days, I remember her showing up that afternoon, standing there with nothing but the clothes on her back. 'Help me. I can't live like her.' Thank God."

Some former fosters move in with siblings who were placed with other families, if those homes have the means and are willing. Some foster parents attempt to offer short-term housing and assist older siblings from other homes with filing for financial aid, getting a job and a car, or otherwise stabilizing their lives into self-sustainability. They do this because of the newly minted adult's connection to their children, as a way of stabilizing the entire family for the benefit of their child. It's something several foster parents mentioned during our talks, that adoption of a child is adoption of her entire circumstances. "Bags and baggage and brothers and sisters and Mom and Dad if they're still around," as one parent put it. "It's all knotted up in the same string."

A few foster kids will be driven to the destination of their choosing and handed a cell phone. Call if you need us, the parents say; we'll come back and get you. Don't stay if you get stuck. Although this sounds good, the kids handed those phones usually won't call.

"It's not like we're stupid," says Angie, who aged out three years ago. "It would be the eight-hundred-pound gorilla in the room. How can they help you if they couldn't afford to keep you? That's my situation. They cried their eyes out when they said goodbye to me. I got a scholarship for my first year of college, and then I dropped out and worked. They wanted to help, but they couldn't, and I just don't want to talk to them about it. They love me, and I love them, so it's not all evil and hard like people want to think. It's no different from my friends with poor parents, just because I was a foster kid. They're fostering another girl now, and I know they'll drive her to college too, if she decides to go. I don't fault them for doing this."

Neither does Cody. "Say parents ask for little kids and plan to adopt them if all goes well. They take teens because that's who's available when they're hoping for somebody younger, or they're in it for the money. The day they can get a kid who's twelve for the same amount of money as a seventeen-year-old eating machine, they boot him and get one. Unless they bond. See, that's something none of us has control over. And no teenager will admit he wants it—not even the eight-year-olds will talk about it—but these kids long for adoption with every fiber of their being. Everything is stacked against them, except human nature to love the underdog, and how bad some people wanna be parents. It's like a human lottery—only so many homes, and within that just so many good ones. But anything can happen. Anything."

In Toby's life as a foster child, anything that could happen, did. His experiences with a failed adoption[8] and a return to foster care encompass many of the elements touched on above. How common are failed adoptions, I wanted to know? One in a hundred, says Dale. One in fifty, says Cassie. Cody shrugs. "It's not common, but they're increasing because of that numbers game we've just been talking about. People don't want to be responsible once the kid turns eighteen."[9]

Born to an alcoholic mother, Toby entered foster care at the age of two. DSS took him to Lisa, herself a former foster child who'd opened up a babysitting service in her home.

"We learned a lot of stuff together," Toby says. "She was my first foster parent. I was her first foster child."

Under court order, Lisa took Toby to regular visitations with his mother. Before he had started kindergarten, he was living a week at a time between Lisa's and his birth mom, Julie's, as she maintained sobriety and sought his return.

Unfortunately, things took a turn for the worse with Julie's new boyfriend, an abusive man. The couple began leaving five-year-old Toby and his infant sister at home alone with no food. One day after school, Toby arrived home to find the boyfriend sitting with his social worker (a woman he barely remembered; "I seen so little of her"). He informed Toby that Julie had been gone a couple of days with no information on her whereabouts, so he'd called the social worker to look after the kids.

Toby went back to Lisa's; his sister went to another foster. Lisa's family, sometimes with temporary fosters from her emergency work, sometimes with just her two bio girls and Toby, took trips to Disney World, to SeaWorld to see Shamu, and to Gatorland, where he still remembers his delight at holding a baby alligator. He made friends from Lisa's babysitting job and in the neighborhood. His best friend lived on a huge farm, and the boys got into mud and ponds, four wheeling and snowboarding together. When he was eight, Lisa asked Toby if he'd like for her to adopt him.

"I didn't know what the word meant. She said, 'I will legally be your mom.' I liked that idea. So we did it. It was all pretty normal there for a while. It wasn't the adoption that started it, but when I was about ten or eleven, Lisa started changing. She seemed angry and depressed a lot."

Toby got into fights at school; his grades were borderline. Things went into a death spiral the first time Lisa received a note from the school about his behavior. She took Toby into a back room and beat him with a belt. As the fights increased and the grades went down, the severity and frequency of the beatings went up. Lisa was a strong and large woman; if Toby sought to elude her or outrun her, she would physically sit on him.

"One time, I remember her laying on me until I literally could not breathe. I was gasping for air, and she looked at me and said, 'Stop faking. I'm not hurting you!' She said stuff like that a lot. I really thought I was going to die that day."

By the time he was thirteen, Toby could physically stand up to Lisa. When he finally told her he'd hit her back if she hurt him again, she eased off. Most of the hitting stopped when her boyfriend moved in, but he and Toby clashed. When Toby was arrested at fourteen for starting a fire at his school, matters came to a head.

"I was proud of myself, getting taken out of the school in handcuffs. See, I was really big into gangsta culture, rap, and all that, so it made me feel like a big man to get arrested. A few minutes later, I was trying not to cry. They called Lisa, and she told them not to bring me home, to take me to jail."

A social worker came to see him there, promising she was familiar with his case. Toby didn't give much credence to her assertion. "I'd seen social workers maybe a half dozen times in my life, despite being on somebody's caseload, I guess. And never at good times."

Toby told her Lisa was abusing him, and she said he was going back into foster care. "That's when I started seeing the good side of foster care."

A few days in a "nice normal foster home" convinced Toby to ask if they'd let him stay. Their answer—a troubled teen couldn't fit into a home with younger children, so sorry, no—gave him his first hard lesson about foster care. One that came a bit late.

"I hadn't thought before that the older you are and the more trouble you've been in, the less people want to let you stay. Hadn't put it together like that. It sounds silly now, but I was fourteen, high all the time, not paying attention." Toby's hair flops into his eyes as he pushes wire-framed glasses up his nose, looking lost for a moment in the memory.

He wound up in Mountaintop Group Home, a facility of eight or so cottages for children of different ages. He had an opening strategy all worked out: "Punch the biggest guy in my cottage, and they would think I wasn't scared." Since Toby turned out to be the biggest kid in the house, he never implemented that plan; he also discovered the place had lax rules. Runaways were accepted back, and it proved easy to walk off for a couple of days, then return. Toby ran away twice during his time there, perhaps as much out of boredom as for any other reason. He also bought pot from his houseparents.

"It all depends on who those places hire," Cody interjects, rolling his eyes. "A good or bad houseparent will make or break you."

During his time at Mountaintop Group Home, Lisa and Toby went to counseling to see if they could reconcile their mother-son relationship and save the adoption. Her attitude confused and annoyed him. "She was always talking about how bad I was; everything was my fault; she hadn't done anything." Years later, Toby would learn that Lisa had been under investigation, about to lose her license to babysit and to be a foster parent, perhaps even headed for prison time. It had been in her immediate best interests to discredit Toby's complaints. Meanwhile, Toby had broken even the lax rules at Mountaintop often enough to be expelled and placed in juvenile detention. After two weeks, his social worker appeared.

"Get in the car. This is your last chance."

Toby asked where they were going.

"Wait and see, but you're not going to like it."

Toby began to get nervous as the town gave way to farms, then forest. They turned up a steep hill. A sign nailed to a tree read "Camp Roaring Fork Outdoor Program."

"I thought to myself, *What have I done?* I had heard rumors of this place. The worst of the worst came here. I went back to my previous strategy: find the biggest guy and punch him in the face. Then figure out how to run away."

The rules were made clear after Toby was searched:

1. Going to school was now a privilege to be earned.

2. Cursing resulted in push-ups and running laps.

3. Smoking and dipping (aka using smokeless tobacco) were also punished.

4. Harder substances were a straight road to Juvie; no second chances.

5. By the way, if he was thinking of picking a fight with the biggest guy in the camp to prove himself, he might like to know that a tent to sleep in was also a privilege he could start earning right then and there by rethinking that plan. Or he could sleep in the open that night. Up to him.

"They could read minds. Not really, but they seen it all before, I guess." Toby's gray eyes widen as he recalls that welcome. "I really was one of those guys who got scared straight."

Thinking that he had just entered hell, Toby was surprised to find camaraderie among the twenty or so boys at the camp. He stayed eleven months, the longest he'd been in one place "since Lisa gave me up."

Near the end of this time, Toby's social worker drove him to a small town. ("It still seemed like New York City to me, after that year in the woods.") A foster family had offered to take fifteen-year-old Toby in. On Sunday, the family went to a local church.

"I went in and seen this amazing girl, but I was too scared to talk to her because I had not spoken to girls in a while. Turned out she was the pastor's daughter, so I figured bad boy here did not have a chance. I left that gangsta mystique in the woods. It was just me wanting to talk to her."

Toby also figured he'd rather stay in the woods than with a foster family, but his social worker wanted to get him back into society, and the camp had already kept him longer than it did most kids.

The DSS worker played a smart card. She set up an introduction between Lindsay, the pastor's daughter, and Toby.

He still laughs, thinking about that "ploy," as he calls it. "We talked for hours. I went back to the woods program for about a week. Then the social worker picked me back up and took me to my new home."

Six months later, Toby had returned to smoking pot and running with a fast crowd. He was also withdrawn and distant with the people in his foster home, and the couple there sat him down to explain their belief that he needed more structure than they could provide.

"Structure didn't enter into it in my mind. I was in love with Lindsay. We'd been dating off and on since I got into that foster home. I begged them to let me stay, but my social worker come and got me and took me to another group home."

The Harvest Home for Boys in Industry Park allowed Toby to continue telephone talks with Lindsay. On his eighteenth birthday, Toby signed himself out of the group home and went to Lindsay's. During those phone calls, which had included Lindsay's parents, they had arranged for their daughter to move in with cousins while Toby stayed with them.[10]

"I got my act together. No more pot, no more gangsta imitations. A real life, being a real man. I wanted to marry Lindsay, and I seen the trust her parents placed in me, taking me into their home. Also, they were checking me out. Was I ready to get married, was I able to do right by her?"

The couple married. Toby joined the army, was medically discharged after a leg injury, and worked various jobs to support his wife and (within three years) two children.

Toby, now in his late twenties, and Lindsay foster a daughter as well. She is the same age as their biological eldest, which "sort of makes it easy, sort of makes it hard. Our daughter showed jealousy at first. Now I think she likes having an ally against their little brother."

From the distance of ten years, Toby looks back on the time when he was aging out. "I didn't have a clue. I didn't have a plan. I wanted my girl, and fortunately her parents seen enough in me to help me help myself. If I hadn't seen her across that church aisle, if her parents hadn't believed in me, if that social worker hadn't set me up, who knows where I'd be? Nah, it ain't the money to go to college or the system or anything but human hearts that gets a messed-up kid straight. That social worker seen me seeing my future wife. Lindsay's dad seen something in me he felt he could work with. Everybody acted on a human emotion. Money didn't enter into it, except that her parents didn't charge me rent or nothing while I lived with them. They helped me become the kind of man they wanted to marry their daughter, because they knew she loved me, and they wanted me to be good enough for her."

One final note on children aging out of foster care: the girls often choose to get pregnant, sometimes while they are still in care,[11] often as soon as they leave adult supervision. It's a deliberate choice that is easy to understand, says Barbie.

"They think that's going to give them unconditional love. We deal with that a lot, from age thirteen and up. It's almost like, if I had a horrible childhood, then forget that. I won't do that to my kid. My kid will love me and not leave me. It divides, too. Boys lean more toward marriage. Girls lean toward pregnancy. We had a girl who came in and got pregnant while still in the system. She has three kids now. She's still under twenty. We deal with that more because there are more girls in foster care already. It's almost that they never felt like they were loved, so they decide to have a child and that's the happy ending. Disneyland, tra-la-la.

"Yes, children are wonderful. But you have to get up and feed them at 2:00 a.m. These kids don't think of responsibility. Why would they? Their parents didn't teach them that. It's their goal to get pregnant. And it all cycles around again. That's why we say, if one of our foster kids raises her own children, she's a success story. Because she is."

10

Cursed Be the Ties That Bind

We had this eight-year-old boy, and he was autistic. This kid was supersmart but socially awkward. I took him and his little sister on a court-ordered visit to his mom, and she's chatting to the girl, trying to engage him, but he's ignoring her, writing on this piece of paper.

She's telling the little girl that she's got a job interview, and if she gets it maybe they can come live with her this summer, and then we're getting ready to go, and the boy hands his mama the paper.

He's made a job application very accurately on this piece of paper—this kid was brilliant—and it's got the blanks for her name and address and the list of questions she has to answer. The first question he asked her is, "Why did you pick drugs over me and my sister?"

The whole application was for returning to being their mom. He hands it to her and walks off. "Bring that next time we meet," he says, and goes and gets in my car.

—social worker

HOPE IS expensive. It eats up a lot of money, time, and emotional energy. The foster care system in America is built on trying to reunite children with parents when possible. That said, a federal law passed in 2008[1] tried to restrict the amount of time children spend in foster care without being available for adoption. Unfortunately, this truncated timeline has produced mixed results because figuring out when a child should go back to one or both birth parents versus when a swift severance is in the best interest of the young'un is a case-by-case decision. What's right for one is wrong for another, and no matter what, somebody isn't going to be okay with the outcome.

Remember Abigail and John? Abigail has advice for prospective adopters entering the foster care system. "Understand that you're not just taking those kids in. You're dealing with their family. Up front or around back, in court or in the community, you're going to deal with the fact that you are parenting other people's kids. At any given moment, your children can disappear out from under you. You love unconditionally, and then they disappear because a judge sent them home. Them's the breaks."

Unconditional love could also include trying to figure out how often the kids should see Bio Mom or Dad, and whether it's helping or hurting, and to what extent the new family can encompass the old one. Boundaries, anyone? Does Bio Mom get invited to Foster Family Christmas dinner if supervised visitation is going well? The unnatural dynamic created between bio and foster mothers is a subject that could fill a library of books. Abigail remains firm: if Bio Mom can safely be part of your child's life, that's best for the child. If she can't, you're going to have to deal with the fact that your child will probably blame you later, as a teen or adult, for not seeing Bio Mom. The ties that bind rarely sever with an adoption.

Here's how a foster child describes the bio connection:

"You feel like your DNA is made up to trust your parents, but then you get jerked out of your home and sent someplace and then back and then someplace else, and you're little, so how are you gonna trust your parents let alone anybody else after that, but you still want to. It's very true, that saying about taking a kid from the bio home opens a wound that will never heal. My mom walked out on me. She told me she was doing it. She took me to a DSS office or something like that; there was a couch in the lobby. And she said, 'Bye!' and went off with her new boyfriend. No, I don't want her back in my life. And still, I think about trying to find her. Which—I kinda hate myself for that."

From his many years of observation, Dale has marked changes. In the 1980s and 1990s, when cases centered on abuse and neglect, attempts to heal the family showed tangible results: get the house cleaned up, install running water, and educate Mom and Dad to employment level.

"We saw places where it could be made better. Drugs are different. Drugs are a scourge, like locusts covering the land. They don't leave much behind. At the same time, now we have therapeutic care, where the most vulnerable children with conditions inflicted on them by drug use can get more help healing. That didn't used to be there."

The involvement of drugs doesn't eliminate reunification as a viable goal. Parents can get sober. About one in twenty does so long-term, gets his or her children back, and stays out of the system.[2] But Dale knows his team is fighting a different war than the one he waged in the seventies and eighties, even the early nineties. Although Oxycontin and its cousins have been around awhile, health experts and journalists alike pinpoint their abuse as exploding in 1996, for a variety of reasons beyond exploration here.[3]

"Drugs have decimated our rural populations. Our health officials call it a lost generation. We have great-grandparents raising children now. As an agency director, my concern is the frail and vulnerable children who come out of that death trap. I don't deal with the sources so much as the results. But unless somebody turns off that tap farther up the line, we're gonna drown down here in coal country."

Despite the horrors that addiction has inflicted on their families, the fact remains that children of addicts still want a relationship with their parents. They may hate them for pushing them into the system. They may hate them more for pulling them in and out of foster homes with "pathetic" attempts to get clean, as one foster child termed it. But they also want a connection, something they can't necessarily define.

"It kills us as functional adults in college," says Susan (the Great Expectations foster child ambassador in Great Rock). "How can we study? Our brains are eaten up with trying to make sense of it all, trying to reconcile what happened to us, redeem it, find the meaning, make it okay. Some of the kids want to talk about what happened to us, and others prefer to carry it inside. There's no right or wrong way to deal with your past. It's up to you."

Susan tells her peers, "'You can talk as much as you want or as little as you want, but what you went through is never gonna be okay.' A lot of kids come in and out of my office, asking me, 'How can I get better? I don't understand why all that happened; I don't know what to do with it.' I tell

them, 'It doesn't get better; just push it off and move on.' Every foster kid
eventually says the same thing: you don't just get over it. You don't heal;
you bury it. Build a wall around it and push it in there and get on with
your life."

Her own advice failed Susan, a story she tells without looking at me.
Her brown eyes stare into the distance as the dim winter's light in her
college office backlights her hair. Susan had always told herself that she
didn't want anything from her birth parents. Her mom lost custody when
Susan was five, and she never knew her father. As her mother tried to get
off drugs and reclaim her daughter, Susan bounced back many times.
Finally, her mother's rights were involuntarily terminated, and Susan was
adopted.

She never looked back—until the day her job at the college in Great
Rock brought interesting gossip on the wind: her mother had remarried.
The man had children, so Susan's bio mom was now raising stepchildren
in a house not far from Bright Camp, the hillside coal camp near Troutdale
which Susan had returned to so often in childhood.

Susan called a friend, and at a time when they knew her mother wouldn't
be there, they drove up to Troutdale and sat across from the new house—a
bungalow across town from Bright Camp, just a few blocks over from the
river. They chose the time carefully.

"I didn't want to see her, but I wanted—I don't know what I was looking
for, I just went up there. We sat in the car across the street, my best friend
and me, looking at the house."

As she talks, Susan begins to articulate, without seeming to know she is
doing it, what she wanted: an answer from her mother on how it was possible to raise someone else's children when she had refused to raise her own.

"I cannot fathom how it's okay with her that she can be a mom now. That's
just crazy to me. I don't know why I went. Closure. It never goes away, that
your mom didn't want you. Like I said, you just build a wall around it and
get on with your life. Otherwise it will eat you from the inside out." Susan
shakes her head.

"Cursed be the tie that binds" is the motto of Linda, a mom at the foster
and adoption support group that Cody's team runs. She and her husband
have three foster kids, ages four, six, and seven. The old family connections
are hardest on four-year-old Brook, Linda feels.

"She only remembers positive things. She remembers her dad lifting her up his shoulders so she could touch the ceiling in her apartment. The rest know that Dad is dead and Mom went to jail, so they can't live with Mom. They all remember they had a baby sister who died related to mom's drug overdose. But the younger one doesn't feel it like the older ones do."

The older children, six-year-old Samantha and seven-year-old Asher, changed the baby's diapers and understood what the arrival of the ambulance and the police meant and how life changed forever. But Brook remembers playing dolls with her mother. When Brook talks with a sense of longing about their family, her older sister Samantha's body language becomes loud: *That's ok; this is good; I'm good here.*

Asher said in counseling that his goal in life was to be in Linda and her husband Mac's family, have a brother and a normal family life, and not have to keep going to counseling or thinking about the past. Linda is under no illusions.

"We're in the process of adopting them, and I know for all that the two older ones say those things, they're going to want to see their mom when she gets out. I've been here before."

The first children Linda and her husband fostered were sisters, ages four and six when they arrived. They were long-term placements with the stated goal of reuniting the family. At first the girls did two weekends a month with Bio Dad, but he disappeared a few months in. Soon after, Birth Mom got clean and sober, so the girls began going back to visit her on the same schedule.

"I have to say unequivocally that I didn't make any of these choices. DSS makes the choices, and they really don't care what you think." Linda pauses. "That sounds bitter. Oh well."

At first, the girls fought physically against the visits DSS ordered them to have with their mother, running away from the car at the last minute, barricading themselves in closets. The youngest child had been sexualized and acted out on visitation days. After copious hours in meetings to implement a family management plan, followed by numerous daytime home visits, then weekends, and an uneventful weeklong stay, the family seemed to be getting back on track. Mom was doing well. No men were hanging around the house. There were no drugs, and discipline did not get out of control. The girls ate regular meals; the water and heat stayed on. Targets were met, threats eliminated, goals achieved.

For Linda, the kicker came when the girls could barely wait to go home for Christmas, a complete flip from the early days when they begged not to see Mom at all. "That made it feel okay." Birth Mom's mother moved in with her, and great-grandma lived around the corner. With this support, the final transition plan was put into place. No one wanted the children's schooling disrupted, and since the bio and foster homes were more than an hour apart, it was agreed to wait until June to send the girls home for good.

Instead, the girls spent weekends and school holidays with Mom; Linda drove them to a store parking lot where they "transferred children between cars," and she picked them up on Sundays.

"We were going to be the next success story. They moved back into the trailer for good in June, and their mama called me every night to say, 'This is what happened today. How do I do this or that? Guess what the youngest said!' It was just amazing, those phone calls. Left me feeling like a million bucks.

"Then over the next year or so it seemed to slide downhill from there, kinda slowly. She's not back into drugs—well, maybe pot—but she had another child just before they went home. They got to hold him the day he was born. Sometimes I kept all three of them on weekends if she'd work extra hours at the hotel. We had a very good relationship, almost like an open adoption. He was an amazing baby boy; I got very attached to him.

"Until recently, I still saw them, gave them school clothes, hand-me-downs from our kids, Christmas presents. My daughter came home from college this past summer, and her first request was to get them to come over so we could take them to the beach. We still have a good relationship with Mom and everybody, but it's very painful because I know it's not a good life for them; there's difficult emotional mental health on the part of Mom, and it's getting worse. That's a tough thing to know."

Although she feels conflicted even to admit it out loud, Linda says she started to step back six months prior to our interview. She told the girls that their mom felt too challenged and that their great-grandma said no when she offered to help out with a couple of things. Linda also made sure the girls knew that she felt their great-grandmother was watching out for Mom, and for the family unity, in a good way. Linda says she feels that DSS tries to do the right things, and that parents' rights are a thin line. She worries that it's not good for the girls to be there with their mother but knows they feel "that biological heart connection. They would protect their mom from us on the phone, on visits, hide her actions. They're so conflicted.

"I've watched it with them, and with the kids we're adopting now. That's why we're adopting them, to cut that bungee cord yanking them back to their bio home without warning. But I still know all these kids have an absolute biological need for their birth family, and I also can see that it's not quite right, but yet they feel loyal. It's not about earned loyalty. It's biology. It's an absolute connection I have to honor."

Linda took in the kids she's now adopting when their mom tested positive at court for drugs and the judge terminated her rights involuntarily. That came after an earlier removal of the children for neglect and endangerment while she was high. Another judge gave her a choice between jail or treatment. She chose rehab, but no beds were available at an appropriate facility. The court said she could go home and call every day until there was a bed available, then check herself in.

With a sharp laugh, Linda asks, "What test do you take to become a judge, anyway? What idiot would think she would do that? They found her in Georgia. She did her time, tried to get the kids back, tested positive in court. It's over for her."

Foster and adoptive parents long to end the harm birth parents cause to their children, and they also have personal feelings invested: ego, love, fear of rejection, and a host of others. Most don't want their children to suffer, and some don't want to suffer because of the other family. None of that changes the fact that eight out of ten former foster children seek out their bio mom (and sometimes dad) as adults.[4]

The bio ties cut both ways. Pam, a colleague at the college where I adjunct in Walker City, called me up one day and asked, "Are you still writing that book about foster kids?"

When I affirmed so, she plunged into her story over the phone. Pam has a sister named Jessie who was deep in drug abuse. Their mother, Donna, clerked for a lawyer in Troutdale who handled state adoptions. One day, Donna received a personal phone call at work. Very personal indeed.

The voice traveling down the telephone line asked if Donna knew that Jessie had given birth to a baby who was immediately taken into foster care? Donna's position meant she had a bit of insight into what to do next.

Pam doesn't know why no one called her mother when they took baby Maggie during Jessie's arrest. "All I know is my niece had been with foster parents for two weeks before we found out."

Donna contacted the appropriate DSS office and was informed that she would need to get licensed as a foster parent, plus petition in family court as the bio grandmother to take the infant from her foster home. The social workers had been told the baby would be available for adoption soon because Jessie's rights were going to be terminated quickly.

Everybody went to court, including the heartbroken couple who had been fostering her. Over the phone line, Pam's voice falters.

"It was horrible. The couple [the foster parents] who had her, they were the sweetest, kindest people. They were who you'd hand-pick to want to raise your child if you weren't going to raise her. But we couldn't leave her there. She was blood."

Maggie is now six, and Nana Donna is her legal mother. Sometimes Pam sees the couple who lost her, in a restaurant or out shopping, and feels "this terrible sensation in my stomach. They didn't deserve to go through that. Somebody made a mistake and let her go, and then she spent two weeks with them. They were in love with her; how could they not be? And then they lost her, and it's because she's ours. We're so happy to have her, but that sucks. We did it. We had to."

11

The Day Barbie Became a Social Worker

*Wouldn't these kids just be better off with their bio parents, people they
at least think love them? At least then they'd see their extended family
on occasion. I didn't use to think like that, not really, but now I say that
because, take the Boss, she doesn't even pretend to love them.*

*It's so disheartening; you try to help, you feel that love and bond with
the children, and you don't understand why the foster parents don't.
Maybe I might feel different if they were my foster children instead of my
cases, but I feel like I'm doing this for the right reasons: I want to help; I
love and care about what happens to these kids.*

*And I get paid shit, and you call me at one o'clock in the morning com-
plaining that your child is hoarding brownies and stealing pencils? And
that's what you're complaining about, and you're getting paid for this?*

—social worker

GIVEN THE condemnation that the public, the foster parents, and the kids
themselves so often heap on social workers, why would anyone become one?

Barbie came to the DSS office that Dale runs when she was a job-
shadowing college freshman. The day Barb declared her intention to become a social worker, Cody took the twenty-year-old aside, "out of Dale's

hearing," and explained why she shouldn't. The hours were long, the pay-check minuscule, the work brutal and unforgiving, with any illusion of being able to engender real change buried under paperwork and regulations and court orders. The parents, the kids, and the public would never understand the pressures but be only too happy to judge her for each and every action.

Worst of all, Barbie would eventually make a mistake. It was inevitable, given that we're all human. But Cody also blamed the heavy workload, the lack of sleep, the demands of the job, and the funding cuts to staff and programming alike.

Cody wipes his eyes. "I told Barb about my buddy Jim. He got named in a lawsuit after the child he left in a foster family over a weekend got sexually abused. He was trying to sort another place out. They knew Jim was getting ready to move him, knew the foster son had requested it and told all sorts of things on them, and I guess that last cork came out of the bottle. They didn't care anymore because he was closing them down. That whole 'there but for the grace of God thing' ain't true. Grace of God or not, everybody's gonna make a mistake, eventually. Being tired, taking your eye off the ball a minute, whatever. It's when, not if. Question is, how bad is it gonna be?"

"He literally cried, trying to stop me," Barbie says. The former DSS intern is now two and a half years into the job—and a whole lot clearer about what brought Cody to tears.

Anger. Reconciliation. Frustration. Hope. "It's not a vicious cycle, but it is a tiring one," Barbie says. Still, she felt drawn to the job. A little secret: if you drill down far enough, most social workers admit to being adrenaline junkies. Drama puts them into overdrive.

Barbie and her colleagues spoke often of the job's excitement factor, never knowing from one day to the next what will be required of them. They recount how their own backgrounds equipped them for a life of guiding and supporting families. Social workers have backgrounds very similar to those of foster parents: some come from stable homes and want to give back, others from chaos they want to redeem.

Newbie and experienced foster care workers alike draw strength and energy from seeing real change in the kids they work with from month to month: improved behavior, realistic approaches to school and their own parents, even physical growth.

"Foster kids are often developmentally delayed physically. Their bodies are under such stress, they can't grow. When they get someplace safe, they blossom, like vines running up a beanpole," says Beth.

It's all worthwhile when you see those changes, Barbie affirms. They keep you going.

"Let me tell you about the day I knew I was in the right place, doing the right thing. It started off pretty badly, actually . . ."

Barbie arrived at her desk a little early one Tuesday, planning to get the notes from the previous night's transport written. She'd taken a young man to a counseling appointment but hadn't yet done the required write-up of time spent with him. Time spent with social workers is always documented, whether regular or therapeutic, although in a therapeutic situation the requirements for notes are much stricter. Barb felt guilty about not having done hers the previous night but figured she had time before her 9:00 a.m. appointment.

At 8:07 her iPhone rang.

"Barbie?" The voice on the other end of the phone was shaking.

"Hi there," she said with a sinking stomach.

"It's Irene. Edna, my birth mother, she stole my credit."

Barb's mind, not yet fueled by a second cup of coffee, scrambled for a foothold. Irene was a seventeen-year-old adopted girl sailing through her junior year of high school, held up as a success story. Barbie had last heard from her when she requested a recommendation letter for a scholarship application. Her new mom, who had other foster children, stopped in the office hallway without fail if she saw Barbie and bragged about Irene's accomplishments at school. Irene's was the kind of adoption that makes social workers feel it is all worthwhile.

Now something seemed a little sideways. "Your mom stole . . ." Trying to catch up, Barbie racked her brains for any gleanings of information on credit theft among fosters. She'd never heard of such a thing. Kids don't have credit, do they? Until recently, foster kids weren't even allowed to have bank accounts.

Irene was still speaking. ". . . and then my social security number. $70,000 in bad debt against my name. She's been at it since I was like five, and I just found out because my mom and dad were going to help me apply for a credit card to establish credit for me. When they said I had a bad credit rating, I went on the site and looked at all the places she's used me to be her. Eleven different states. What do I do now?"

Barely two years into social work, Barb had never felt more like a newbie than in this moment. She had no idea what Irene should do next. Hovering in the back of her mind was the awareness that Irene was technically no longer on her caseload because her adoption had gone well and removed her from the books. Barb dismissed that thought almost before it formed. This kid had been making it; if she needed help, she would get it. Why did bad stuff keep happening to good kids?

Barb breaks from her story for a moment and laughs, holding up one finger. "I've learned not to ask that question." Then she returns to her tale.

"I don't know at this minute, Irene. Lemme check some things out with my supervisor and get back to you. Is this the number where I can reach you?"

Gulping the rest of her coffee, Barb walked to Dale's office. She found the boss, mug in hand, perusing field notes from other caseworkers. Barbie realized that she had left her computer screen open mid-notes, a bad thing to do. *Firing offense* ran through her brain, but this would just take a second. She outlined Irene's call.

Dale leaned back in his chair and threw his head against the seat with a dramatic sigh. "Not again."

"This happens often?" Barb asked.

"Too often." Her supervisor sat upright again. "Right, there isn't a lot we can do. But there's an online group that supports kids going through this process, and she needs to request a credit freeze until she gets this sorted out. She'll need hard proof, like a bill in her name. If she has that, and she's willing, she can file a police report against her birth mother. Not all kids are willing to do that. Whether she is or not, she needs to call the Identity Theft Resource Center."

Writing furiously, Barb thought to herself that, of all the kids she knew, Irene would be the one most willing to file against her bio mom. Animosity would have been a polite term for what the teenager felt toward her birth mother.

Dale paused, then added, "Not that it's much consolation, but tell her that about one case in twelve of credit fraud nowadays involves somebody under the age of eighteen. Sometimes it's kids who live in their own birth homes."

Barbie shook her head. "That's low. A mean thing to do. Not a small number."

Dale smiled. "I knew what you meant. Good luck to her. She's, ehm, not actually one of your kids, is she?"

Shrugging, Barbie avoided eye contact with her supervisor. Dale nodded, leaned his chair forward again, and put his hands on the keyboard. "Don't worry. Tell her to call the Resource Center, and wish her luck from all of us. Poor kid thought her troubles were over, and now this?" He shook his head and returned to his paperwork.

Back at her desk, Barbie hid her screen, then called and passed the information about the Identity Theft Resource Center to Irene. At the end, she said, "Honey, if I can help further, let me know how. I haven't dealt with this before, but this will likely be a long, drawn-out process."

Irene's gulp was audible. "But I need to get a student loan for college. This won't be fixed by then, will it? It can't be. The companies are gonna want their money; they don't care who racked up the charges, do they? A lot of it is like utility bills and stuff."

"Don't borrow trouble," Barbie started, but stopped when Irene barked with laughter. "Ummm, bad choice of words. See how far you can get with that Resource Center. Ask people at your support group if they've dealt with this. They may have ideas about how you can find old bills and other proof."

"I don't know why I'm surprised she did this," Irene said, as if she hadn't heard. "She is all about her; she always has been and always will be. I don't know why I didn't see this coming. It happened to a friend of mine from group therapy. She told us about it. Why didn't I check then? Not that it would have made any difference. Aaagh, it just seems like every time I make a plan, there's something from my past blocking it."

"I hear you. Check what the Center has to say. If I can help, call me back."

She glanced at her watch. 8:45. Five minutes to finish working on the notes before she had to leave for her appointment. Sighing, she saved the file and closed it. Five minutes wasn't worth the effort.

Her 9:00 a.m. appointment was with Jack, a twelve-year-old boy working on his sixth foster home. Not used to structure but very accustomed to exhausting others' benevolence, Jack had a pattern common to many bouncers: pull all the behavioral tricks out of his bag early on to see how fast he could get the new families to give up on him. His last placement had requested he go after fifteen days.

"That's what happens when a five-foot-ten beanpole of a boy gets up on a stool and pees into the sink during dinner," Dale said at the previous staff meeting—the one at which he assigned Jack to Barbie.

Barb needed the extra time, as she and Jack would be having breakfast together before she drove him to a psychiatric appointment, then to an eye exam, and then back to his foster home. The family—Jack, his fostering parents, and twin sisters in the process of being adopted by the parents—were going to Dollywood the next week. Jack didn't want to go.

"I could stay in respite care. I could stay in a group home. Why should I get dragged around this place with a couple of babies and have to do everything they wanna do, just because they're getting adopted? They're just trying to get them to like them." From the backseat—Jack refused to sit up front—the teen growled a running commentary of complaints.

Barb glanced in the mirror; Jack's arms were crossed, his face a study in stubbornness. She sighed. "You know, lots of kids would jump at this chance. They're not gonna make you do everything the girls want to do. I'm sure Seth will go on a few rides with you while the girls hang with Mona."

The derisive snort emanating from the backseat rivaled that of a grown horse. "Those girls are all over Seth, all about him. It's like they ain't never had a daddy before. Nothing from the time he gets home 'til they go to bed but 'Play with us; watch this; do that!' Makes me sick. Surprised he don't take those girls to bed with him."

"It might be time for an attitude adjustment," suggested Barbie as they turned into the parking lot of Hardee's.

"Don't you start lecturing me," Jack snarled.

"This isn't a lecture. It's a pep talk. Have you ever been to Dollywood?"

Jack cut his eyes away. Barb let it go until they ordered—which went something like this:

"What would you like to eat, Jack?"

Shrug.

Smiling at the elderly woman behind the cash register, Barb said, "I'll have the Chicken Biscuit combo with a large coffee. Would you like a bacon and egg biscuit, Jack?"

Jack crossed his arms again.

"He'll have bacon, egg, and cheese, with a Coke."

"I want a sausage biscuit and hash browns." Jack spoke directly to the counter server, who looked at Barbie with something between confusion and annoyance. Barb deepened her smile into an apology.

"Void that last bacon biscuit," the counter worker threw over her shoulder to coworkers. "I need a sausage."

After they sat, Barb tried again. "The family wants you to have a good experience. Want to know what my favorite ride is at Dollywood?"

"No. They want me to have such a great experience, why don't they adopt me too, not just the girls?"

Unbidden, Barb remembered her childhood, sitting silently at the table while her younger sister dominated the conversation, telling their parents about her day, bright, proud, and confident. She took up most of the oxygen in the room—any room.

Personal history gets left outside the workday, she heard the voice of one of her professors. They all tended to blend together now. She returned to the moment.

"Jack, going to Dollywood is not punishment. It's fun. Think about enjoying it?"

Jack took a huge bite out of his biscuit, a noisy slurp of Coke. "Bunch of baby shit."

"Attitude adjustment," Barb repeated. "A chance to go someplace you've never been and try some fun stuff. Could it be like that?" She spent the next ten minutes describing roller coasters and waterslides as Jack sat, picking the sausage out of his biscuit, flicking hash browns off the table, and slurping soda.

A week later, Jack burst out of the house to their breakfast meeting and narrated in hand-waving detail all the wonders of his family trip: the stuffed animal he won at a gallery and Seth's complimenting him on his shooting; the street magician who asked him to help pull a rabbit out of his hat and then gave him a rubber magic wand; Foster Mom's offer for everyone to choose T-shirts at the souvenir stand. "She said we could have whichever we wanted. They got pink, but I got a black one." He also belched loud enough to cause the Hardee's manager to cast an eye on the table, and flicked hash browns.

Barb would pass a truncated version of this narrative on to coworkers at a staff meeting, along with a vivid description of her "attitude-adjustment pep talk" that made everyone laugh out loud. Then Dale, as is his way, brought the teaching point to a head.

"It pays to remember that foster kids are kids first. In this case, a teenager with the same attitudes and annoyances as every other wing-testing man-child in the land. Contrariness comes with the territory. Good job, Barb."

Telling the story now, Barbie tosses her hair and all but smirks. "And right after that, Irene's family had a friend who's a hotshot lawyer. He took her case pro bono. She got her credit score cleared in time to go to college. That didn't have anything to do with what I did, I know. But it was rocket fuel in my motor. Bad deal fixed for a good kid. So maybe being a social worker isn't for everyone. But it's for me."

Dale smiles at how Barb drew inspiration from these events. He's glad to hear of their refueling effect because one of the most significant qualities this field veteran sees in his best workers is endurance.

"What makes a good foster parent makes a good social worker. Are you in it for the long haul? Anybody can show enthusiasm for six months. Altruism dies. What's buried deep comes out, and then it gets real. Nobody's still here after a couple of years unless they really get it."

What does "getting it" entail? Those who stay the course love working with the kids (or even love the kids, all of them, with no overt favoritism). They have a compassionate orientation about life in general and realistic expectations about how much people can change. They have "minimal" control issues.

"All social workers have control issues or they wouldn't be taking a job that constantly requires them to change things for the better," says Dale. "We're looking for the ones who can harness that personality quirk for the greater good."

And while their personalities may be strong, social workers are not dominators.

"There really aren't a lot of alpha males and queen bees—boy, I hope that's not sexist—in social work, not long term." He chuckles suddenly. "A lot start that don't finish."

Also, not to put too fine a point on it, social workers who last have good supervisors. One of the reasons he's so beloved by his former therapeutic community was Dale's determination as their supervisor to keep caseloads to a maximum of seven per worker. That's a luxury supervisors in DSS don't have. While every child who needs foster care must be taken into the system, a supervisor can refuse to classify a child as therapeutic if there's no caseworker with an open slot in his subcontracted agency. There is always a waiting list for the designation. Dale understands that this protectiveness made him a target of criticism, but he is proud that his protégé Cody maintained it when he became supervisor.

"Therapeutic is different for a reason; that's the whole point. This is a hard job, keeping up with the most vulnerable of those already vulnerable. Caseworkers need someone to watch their backs. Not too many cases to reasonably handle; how can they keep up with what's going on if there's no time to schedule visits?

"Don't forget, there's riding herd on the foster parents. We tend to think if it's quiet, that's good. Not necessarily true in this line of work. Sometimes what drives people to become foster parents makes them unable to ask for help. They can't stand the idea of failure. You've got to be proactive when you don't hear from them. How can you do that if your caseload is too heavy?"

A DSS worker gives a snort of pure frustration. "We think the same. But we still have to take every case assigned us, and we still get it in the neck when we can't keep up."

Dale cuts her a sympathetic look, then casts his gaze to the carpet. "Nobody said life was fair. But if we don't watch over them, who's going to?"

12

The Day Beth Stopped Being a Social Worker

Most of the parents start off meaning well and go dark. Around here there's not a huge pool to choose from, and yet we have so many children in need, we let things slip by. I went to a meeting with a bunch of other caseworkers from another county, and someone raised her hand and said to the DSS director at the meeting, 'I think we should do mental-health evaluations on applicants.' He dismissed it because, he said, we wouldn't have any applicants.

—*social worker*

THE DAY Beth believes was "the beginning of the end" of her career as a social worker started with a phone call. "The foster mom called to tell me this boy had to be removed from her home right that minute, and I could hear a woman yelling in the background, literally screaming, 'You pervert!'"

When Beth arrived, the family told her that the foster mom's granddaughter, four years old, had been sitting on their kitchen counter. She said she wanted down. Their foster son, a teenager, lifted her around her waist and lowered her to the floor.

But when he did, the biological child of the house said to him, "Don't do that." The little girl's mother began screaming that he'd hurt her and yelling at her mother that her foster child had hurt the baby, that he was a pervert.

"That's what I heard when the foster mom called me. She was the grandmother of the little girl. So off that kid goes, in the backseat of my car, clutching his black garbage bag against his stomach. Now what? He's been labeled as acting out sexually. With Mom and Grandma in the room, and they can't see how simple that was? Some kinda family dynamic was at play between the mother and daughter, and he got dragged into it."

That boy—"Branded with an F-for-foster on his forehead so he couldn't be this nice kid who was just helping the little girl down, could he?"—was on Beth's mind the best part of the week.

"That grandma had been a really good mom to the boy—I'd heard her tell him she loved him— and then the moment something happened, it was like he didn't mean anything to her. How can you just switch it off? That's of concern to me."

The sexual innuendo was not. Beth and her colleagues have repeatedly dealt with parents and a public eager to categorize foster kids as sexualized.

"News flash: All boys will eventually masturbate. If you don't want a masturbating child in your house, don't foster a boy. But if you're foster-ing one, and your washcloths start disappearing, don't call me and say he's stealing them. Get a clue. I had a mom with a bio son who was fostering two teen boys the same age, and she called to say they were using them for toilet paper—she kept finding them in the trash can.

"She got so mad at them, and I'm trying to tell her leave them in the trash, don't make a big deal out of it. In this case, it was just healthy boys doing the usual exploration, but if it had been sexualized kids, you don't want to perpetuate the damage. This is progress; go out and buy cheap washcloths."

Beth laughs. "It would be funny if the stakes weren't so high. Age-appropriate exploration is a normal part of human development. In a kid who really has been sexualized, it's also damn healthy. Her son wasn't old enough for her to know about that period in a boy's life yet. The good thing about her was, when I finally got through to her, she didn't blame them for dragging her son into it. She just said, 'Oh! Okay, but I'm buying them pink washcloths.'" Beth laughs again. "That foster mom actually had a good sense of humor. She was just naïve."

While the second mom laughed off her suspicions once they were explained, the first wasn't prepared to see her charge as innocent until proven guilty. On the heels of that removal came another difficult case.

Jody had lived since the age of six with Peggy, a single mother who adopted him "in the cute sweet years when they hang on you and say, 'Thank you.'" Jody was about fourteen when he came into Beth's caseload as a normal transfer from a retiring coworker. Life progressed with little drama; Beth had occasional meetings with Jody, and no alarm bells rang. Peggy's daughter, two years older than Jody and in dual enrollment at college, encouraged him to think about college himself, but he had trepidations. Beth chipped away at this reluctance during each visit.

But when Jody was seventeen, Peggy kicked him out of the house and called Beth on her iPhone.

"Her exact words, sailing out of a clear blue sky, were, 'He and his shit are in the garage; I don't care what you do with him, but you better come get him.'"

The story unfolded in bits and pieces, cobbled together from Peggy's enraged accusations and a visit to the school to pull Jody out of class (he was not, in fact, in the garage) and fill in the missing parts. Peggy had secreted cash in her house—$14,000 to be exact, hidden in a shoebox under her bed. When it went missing, she accused her son, and Jody fessed up; he'd been giving money out at school, wanting to show his peers that he had some, that he wasn't "just a poor foster kid with nothing of his own." He'd also been meeting his bio parents and had given them most of Peggy's cash. His father had contacted him through Facebook.

Children longing for a genuine relationship with birth parents often try to jumpstart one by complying with their requests; Jody was no exception. When Peggy booted him, her daughter remained in the house, even though it turned out that Jody had given her a couple thousand dollars of the money. Peggy didn't see that as a double standard. Jody was leaving; that was that.

"You adopted Jody; he's as much yours as your daughter is," Beth argued.

"No. She's flesh and blood. If this is the way he treats me, he's done living here."

Beth interrupts her story to sit silently for a moment, then says. "That stuck to me, how she said that."

Jody went to stay with a biological brother's adoptive family. They took him in even though they received no stipend for his care. Peggy continued to receive Jody's adoption subsidy, probably feeling entitled to it to make up for her missing cash. The hosting family didn't contest the arrangement.

Peggy also went to court to terminate her rights as Jody's mother. She told the judge her former son was no longer welcome or trustworthy. When the ad litem pointed out that prelicensing advice to foster parents includes locking away valuables, Peggy said that it was her home, and she could have cash in it if she wanted to.

In his ruling, the judge said something else that stuck in Beth's mind.

"This is not the pound; you can't just return what doesn't work out. I'm not granting a termination here. Work it out."

Jody stayed where he was without support, and the family struggled to keep the brothers in enough food to satisfy the teen boys' appetites. Peggy visited sometimes, bringing him new clothes and some items left behind after she kicked him out. She also made him work off the money taken by doing odd jobs around her house. Jody moved back in with her briefly after he graduated from high school, but he didn't stay long.

"I don't think he ever got over knowing she valued that money more than him. He heard in court what she said about her birth daughter. His father was famous in the community for drugs and homelessness, swindling, pretty much living off the streets. After he got the money, he took off again. That made it like a one-two punch for Jody. His birth family didn't care, his bio dad used him, and then his mom, who adopted him from fostering and said every day since he was six that she was going to take care of him for life, wouldn't let him back in the house after he made a stupid mistake. Not until he'd paid it all off by working for her.

"Throughout those years, how often did she say she loved the child, tell him, 'I'm giving you a good home; I want you to do better; I care about you'—but when it really mattered, there was never a bond. Not a real one. I think that got to me more than anything else I'd seen, how easy it was for her to turn her back."

Beth has seen other parents refuse to turn their backs, even under great provocation. Take the sweet, loving couple who opened their home to a foster son, aged eight. Benny took the coloring sheets they gave him each day with a shy smile of thanks, went to his room, pooped on them, and slid them behind his dresser. It took a couple of weeks for Foster Mom to catch up with what was happening, but eventually . . .

Time to bring in some creative parenting strategies. Overwhelmed and shaken by what they could not categorize in terms of motivation, those parents hoped Benny might have a medical issue and asked for help in making appointments via Medicaid. When the social worker heard the problem, she winced. Benny was from a home where a toilet had not been part of his upbringing. No running water. Sanitation not a priority. Living in a corrugated shed. He'd been used to defecating outside on the ground. The whole carpet and bedroom thing was new for him, and nobody had taught him the toilet's magical properties.

Nobody except the social worker could have known he didn't already understand them. For some reason, the parents hadn't been fully informed before they took Benny—probably because the responsible person, feeling overwhelmed with other duties, had accidentally (or perhaps deliberately) neglected the part that could have been a deal breaker. Or maybe the social worker didn't know. It's a chaotic system. Information sometimes gets lost in the shuffle.

Beth sighs. "We got that straightened out. But it's hard for people to realize what foster kids don't know. That particular case, we'd say, was a little extreme, but most foster kids have never eaten at McDonald's, don't remember having a Halloween costume, never hunted an Easter egg. They missed out on normal, age-appropriate kid stuff, and it's not their fault. Foster parents can't believe a child's naïveté about chores or hygiene when they know so much about sex and drugs."

It's an unfortunate circumstance, says Beth, because for all the hard work, fostering can be a real joy, and she's been "blessed and reenergized" every time a foster parent has discovered this seam of happiness inside the mountainous work of child-rearing.

"It's like they're unprepared to find joy in the sweet simple side of the job—take the kid trick or treating, give them a childhood—because they're freaked about the sexualized stuff. Now tell me how you're gonna make these kids worse off by getting involved, once you know that. People say that all the time: they're afraid to foster because they'd mess the kids up worse than they already are. How can you break something that's already smashed?"

Beth launches into another story, about an older woman fostering a young boy. He was about ten when placed with her, and not twenty-four hours later, Beth's phone rang.

"Come get this child; he's nasty and disrespectful." Beth asked why, and it turns out she'd given him some sheets and told him to make his bed, but he'd slept on the bare mattress.

"This freaked her out, hygienically speaking." Beth sighs. "I don't mean to make fun of her. People are gonna think she was at fault. She wasn't; well, she was, but it looked like an easy fix."

Beth suggested the lady make the bed with him once, showing him how. She responded, "He's ten years old and won't make his own bed? This is defiance. It's not like I'm loading him down with chores. He won't even dust."

"I had to assure her that putting sheets on a bed was, in fact, beyond the knowledge of this boy, and could she please show him how to do it? And finally it kind of got through to her. I think she was embarrassed then, touched—she sounded like she was gonna cry—but also so startled she couldn't admit it."

The "he's disrespectful and he won't dust" story would be funny if it didn't reflect dire circumstances. The foster mom had told the boy to use Pledge when he dusted, and he put his hand on his heart and started reciting the Pledge of Allegiance to the American flag.

"Let me guess; he didn't do chores a lot?" the foster mom asked when Beth laughed at this story, then caught herself and explained.

"And where this boy lived, how he lived, I just said, 'You got it.' And she kinda did. At least she could hear me and change her mind. I didn't have to pull that kid out of another home."

When foster parents expect their new family members to do chores they've never learned in previous houses, they have to teach them from the beginning. But it's not just chores; it's life skills, such as those Annie tried to instill in Dana and her sisters. And it is fun stuff. The beach is one of many experiences that foster kids miss out on, not to mention learning to ride a bike, cook, drive, swim, knit, ride a skateboard. "They didn't get much childhood, and the pieces of it they did get don't fit together. They just need childhoods."

It sounds succinct when Beth puts it that way, but foster parents can get pretty ticked off when talking about what the social workers don't tell them regarding the children they've taken in. They know they're going to have to learn most things about their child's past by dealing with them directly, but they'd rather not. It's frightening. It doesn't feel best for the child. It wastes time and energy.

Beth praises that couple who took Benny. "Everybody knew they were good parents. That may be why Benny went there."

But his foster mom is not having it. "They could have told us to teach him about toilets, and we would have. They just didn't want to tell us."

It's a fair complaint, says Beth, but sometimes, rather than being afraid to point out a deal breaker, social workers really don't have many details to tell. She doesn't know which was true for that particular child but puts the odds at fifty-fifty.

Part of Beth's shock at Peggy's response was that she hadn't considered the older woman one of the mediocre homes. When the going gets tough, they quit. But the "good" parents?

"Once, not long after I started, I had to go to school and remove a kid from his foster home straight from school. At the request of the foster mom. I can't even tell you why now. But she packed his stuff while he was gone, the stuff she was willing to let him take. Sometimes they won't let the kids take things they've bought since they were there; it varies from house to house. And I took his stuff in the garbage bag in my backseat and picked him up at school and said, 'Guess what, we've got a great new placement for you tonight!' Because I'd had enough warning to find one." Beth looks away.

"After a while, you don't believe anybody, and then you should probably get out."

Peggy reinforced for Beth a lesson she thought she'd learned: it's hard to tell what the true motivations of the human heart are when tested by extreme provocation and given chances to opt out. But as bad as the dynamic surrounding Jody's theft felt, Beth believes it was the boy at the countertop who became the proverbial straw on her overloaded social worker's back.

"I couldn't get out of my head how much she'd promised this kid, and how little she delivered, and why did she act like that? Her daughter manipulating her, her wanting to get a different foster kid in because she wanted to adopt a girl—somebody said that—just whatever. It didn't matter. I started applying for jobs."

Dale has seen his fair share of social workers come and go. People might be inclined to believe that good social workers get worn down, jaded, and cynical from the demands of working in a system that doesn't give them the time or resources to do their jobs and doesn't have rules that are geared toward the safety of the children. In reality, Dale thinks good social workers don't turn into bad ones. They quit instead.

"Someone who enters this profession with a poor work ethic will eventually make a bad mistake or get fired. Or they won't, and they'll get promoted and retire. I've seen both. The really good ones might go cynical, but they don't get ground down. They keep fighting for the kids until the day they retire, or they decide to walk away. They've got too much integrity to stay in the job and become part of the problem, so they quit."

Beth now works in legal services, where her history in foster care makes her a valued specialist in the office. "I can still fight for the kids from the legal-system angle. And I still think about the kids, the ones I had, and the ones I never even met, out there floating around, waiting for some adult to notice them and care."

And sometimes, at the grocery store or out to dinner with her husband, Beth hears from someone else's phone the ringtone that was on her work phone. The one she had to answer within fifteen minutes, ready to help the parents through whatever was on the other side.

"Even though I know in my head that's not for me, the pit drops out in the bottom of my stomach, my hands shake, and I start to sweat. It's like PTSD."

13

Why People Don't Foster, and Why They Do

You get these kids, and they're already twelve, thirteen years old, and they've never had anybody on their side before. No one cared what they got on their report card or what they wore to school. They're not ready for you to be asking them questions or showing interest. They can get confused. You have to let them come to you. But they also blossom.

We had a girl come stay with us, maybe our sixth foster daughter. Some had moved on. And this girl, hard as nails. Didn't care what happened, didn't care about anything or anyone, and most important didn't believe we cared about her.

We're not even a week in, and I get this call from her school: she's sassed her teacher; she's got detention. She comes home; I confront her; she's all "Why do you care? You're just looking for an excuse to dump me." And I say, "Next time you do that, there will be consequences, but it won't be dumping you."

Of course, she does it again; and the day after that I drive her to school, and I park the car and go into the building with her. And she says, "What are you doing?" Like I'm killing her.

"I'm going to school with you. If you can't behave like a young adult, I'll sit with you until you can." And I went to all her classes, just sat there next to her, and that child did not open her mouth all day long except to say, "Yes, ma'am. No, sir."

Next day I asked her, "Can you handle behaving like a responsible adult on your own, or do you need help again?" And she said she thought she could handle it. She never acted out to a teacher again—not that I heard about, anyway. And her grades improved. She brought home her report card, and I fussed over it, told her how proud we were she'd done so well, and she just beamed. That's what happens. You see these kids come out of themselves, turn into who they want to be, if you just show them you care. But you've got to invest in it. I had to take the day off and show her—and her school—that I meant business, that I was paying attention. Once they knew that, we were off to the races.

—foster mom

COALFIELDS APPALACHIA is no stranger to need. But foster care and adoption programs are unique within the region in that such great piles of funding exist to assist with them. Given the seven fairly well-staffed private organizations, the multiple (short-staffed) DSS offices, and the fact that everyone across America knows about the drug crisis fueling foster care needs, why aren't more people of compassion genuinely interested in being foster parents—in Coalton or anyplace else?

Three big reasons come up again and again, social workers and fosters parents agree. And while I'm not looking at the big national picture, these don't seem to be Coalton-specific. At national conferences, social workers compare stories on recurring themes:

1. "I never thought about it."

2. "I'd mess the kids up."

3. "I don't have the time / money / ability."

And the "unspoken" reasons:

4. The system treats kids like yo-yos, and I'd get attached and go crazy.

5. The kids are too scary (aka the "demon seed" excuse).

It is a happy thing to observe that the first two reasons people give are about awareness issues—until you find out how much money has been

spent on making people aware, with how little result. Without giving specific numbers by program or state, masses of funding have gone into foster
care awareness campaigns from DSS or agencies contracted for therapeutic
care. Odds are good that right now you're remembering a billboard or a
wicket sign you've seen while driving around Tennessee, Virginia, West
Virginia, Kentucky, or North Carolina. The advertising is intense.

Cody is all over recruitment and positivity campaigns as part of his
supervisory duties. He holds regular events throughout his service area:
art shows at libraries, guest speakers at churches and schools, and open-
invitation events "any place that'll have us."

Making foster kids visible in a positive way helps get the word out about
fostering and adoption through the state system or its private subcontrac-
tors. People know about international and private adoptions, but they
seem to be much less informed about state-sponsored adoptions.[1] Public
activities also combat the negative stories that feed into that belief that
foster kids are some form of "demon seed." (This is a term that many social
workers use when describing public attitudes.)

That's the kind of eye-opening Cody loves to bring about. At Great
Rock's library, he and some colleagues recently organized an art exhibit
featuring young adults who aged out of foster care; the artists came to
the library at the display's culmination and discussed their sculptures and
what they symbolized. His enthusiasm for the project was aimed at reason
number five people don't foster, the "demon seed" idea.

"That way people come and listen and see they're not cat-killing, fire-
setting devil worshippers. They're kids in the community with jobs and
college plans, just like everybody else, with baggage. They just had the bad
luck to get too old in foster care to be cute and adorable at the adoptable
stage and aged out in a group home or a permanent placement."

Cody also oversees the weekly support group that runs in the Industry
Park office. Everyone in the system urges parents interested in going into
fostering to seek out a support system, formal or informal. Cody tries to
make sure there's one in every corner of his service area.

"One of the best things we ever did is start those groups," says Cody.

His agency holds these foster- and adoptive-parent meetings so parents
can interact, talking over what's going right and wrong. Parents may talk to
a nurse brought in at their request to address the group, or swap strategies

with each other for preventing bedwetting. The kids play in the gym while the parents chat about school and community pressures.

It's good for everybody, but particularly for the kids, says one mom. "We feel very supported; we've got our family around us here plus this group, but these gatherings really help the kids, socially. They love being in a group where they're like other people. When we started, I wondered how they would feel about going to something like that, but they love being with those who've had similar life experiences. They go home, and their behaviors improve. That was something else I worried about; would they trade tips for driving all us adults crazy? But they just love being around other kids who can relate to them."

A foster dad from the support group offers temporary placements to babies born addicted; he says his phone rings "nonstop," and he can't imagine not having the group to talk to.

"Nothing prepares you for that moment when you get the phone call, and you race to the hospital, and this waif is lying there, all helplessness and big eyes, screaming his lungs out."

Drug babies scream "a lot." They are so overstimulated by everything around them that it becomes difficult to comfort them without adding to their pain.

"You're trying to love them, but you have to be so careful. It tears your heart out, and then that little baby will tear up your home, your marriage, and your sanity, unless you're prepared to be more than a bleeding heart. Have people you can talk to, or you will go crazy. Not just for advice, but for support. Two different things."

Among the topics of lively discussion I observed among parents at the Industry Park office meetings: IEPs (Individualized Education Plans for developmentally delayed children—almost all foster kids, even those with intelligence in the "gifted" range, are behind in some area of educational, emotional, physical, or social development); sibling rivalry; and doctors who violate blended-family etiquette and privacy. The story of one twelve-year-old's discovering she was adopted because a visiting pediatric specialist from University City told her still circulates, eight years after the incident. The specialist knew the girl didn't know but told her because "you're old enough to know, and your parents shouldn't be keeping it from you." Perhaps the word *hicks* hovered in the background. No lawsuit resulted, but some policy changes rippled through the hospital system, and future visiting pediatric specialists were forewarned.

The primary focus of the support group is indeed to provide a safe place for interaction among foster and adoptive parents, Cody says, but there is a second reason, tied to his outreach and recruitment strategy.

"It doesn't matter what I tell people at an information session about what it's like to foster. When I look at my active roster of foster parents, all but one in the whole service area is there because he or she knew someone else fostering first."

The team is always looking for good fosters who can bring in more, role models who bring in other good people and teach their friends by example not to believe what they read or hear.

Cody shakes his head in exasperation. "If I believed every lie people told about that 'demon seed' idea in our kids, or the big news stories spread about this and that corruption in the system, I'd shoot myself. But it just kills recruitment. People don't tell us they're afraid of the kids. What they say is, 'I'm afraid I'd mess them up worse than they are.' Which is a round-about way of getting to 'these kids are messed up.'"

Perhaps this is where time commitment enters the equation, hitting that third reason why people don't want to foster. It is often referred to as parenting on steroids, and as many foster parents told me over and over, it takes a lot more time to parent someone else's birth children than to parent your own.

Beth underlines the importance of time. "You have to supervise the kids, not leave them unattended or in situations where their triggers are likely to be exploited. We stress twenty-four/seven supervision. We know you have to go to the bathroom, you have to sleep some time, but don't put yourself or other children in the home in situations where they can act out. Don't leave them alone. If they're not supposed to share a room, don't let them. Have a rule in the house that all doors are open unless you're peeing or taking a shower."

Foster children with issues aren't evil; they've acquired behaviors picked up by observation or through survival instinct in a difficult home. But their natural behaviors can be startling to parents unprepared to rethink what childhood looks like for some. Beth remembers the turbulent foster placement and equally unhappy removal of brothers whose bio family had sexualized them. They weren't meant to share a room, but their foster mother grew tired of enforcing that discipline. She also didn't see the need for it.

"I think she thought we were being cruel or weird. She said to me, 'They like to sleep together at night; what's the big deal?' Let me just tell you, if a social worker is stipulating dos or don'ts for a child, it's for a reason. It's not to make it harder being parents; we already know that's tough. We ask you to bring children into your home that are not yours, care for them like they're your own, but don't get attached because at any time they might get yanked into a family placement or back to Mom. So if we say something does or doesn't need to happen, it is for a good reason. That story about the brothers does not have a happy ending."

Sexualized behaviors fall into the "demon seed" category and require a high time commitment from foster parents. It is less a question of lifelong damage to that child than of retraining. Of course sexualized behaviors are undesirable when fitting children out for life but not any more so than the other inappropriate things they need to relearn. It takes time and consistency to remove these behaviors, but time is also on the foster or adoptive parent's side.

Although Margie and Sandy had resisted having a sexualized child in their home because their youngest birth child, Glen, was just eight years old, she came anyway, at the age of four.

Margie gives a lopsided grin, tilting her head. "They were siblings. We couldn't say we weren't taking the youngest one because she'd been sexualized. We gave in."

For the most part, wee Melody's sexualized remarks flew over Glen's head. Margie came in for more of its impacts. One day, as Margie lay on the couch reading a book, young Melody climbed up and started moving her pelvis against Margie's, saying, "This is how people have sex."

Margie replied, "That is more or less correct. And I don't want to, so stop, please."

Melody jumped down and asked for a snack. Within months, her activities with social peers crowded out her age-inappropriate knowledge.

"She got bored with it, the way kids do with most things." Margie shrugs. "You don't lose your cool, you don't go into 'How could she know this?' You just divert them into productive paths. They're kids. It's parenting. Foster care is parenting on steroids, but it's still parenting."

When she and Sandy began, Margie had in mind that they would serve as role models for those around them, influencing colleagues toward foster care. People with adopted children don't introduce them as adopted, particularly not in front of the kids; when Margie was at a family day for work over the summer and people looked at the stair-step six, knowing she had only had three the year before, she was ready with an explanation.

"We have six children, ages five to nineteen. Three of them came from my body."

A good line works miracles. Colleagues previously unaware of the family's expansion assured her they understood. One of her department associates has children adopted from extended family members. But as time wore on, neighbors and others in Margie and Sandy's circle seemed to resist conversation. Margie started to worry that her coworkers whispered condemnation behind her back for "doing that to my kids, my bio kids."

Margie explains, "More people should and could do this, and they're not. I really think people, unfortunately, in my part of society—my class, education level, income bracket, if you want to call it that—they worry too much about messing up their bio kids, what effect the new kids will have. And I did worry, to an extent. We said, 'We're not taking any sexualized kids'—and then, of course, we did. But originally I said we don't wanna deal with that, don't wanna hear it. That's a struggle; people worry, and it's a justified concern—but also, it's a teaching opportunity for kids already in a family to be aware that these kids have had a hard time because of circumstances beyond their control."

Margie firmly believes that her bio kids have benefited more than not, primarily through seeing how privileged they are to have an intact family, supportive parents who give them what they need, and a lot of what they want, plus love. Before the family took on long-term fostering, Margie and Sandy did respite care. Although those children were in the home for only a week to a month, they knew they weren't staying, so they told the bio kids all sorts of things. From these stories, and from seeing social workers and hearing about court appearances, Margie felt her bio kids knew from an early age that "not everybody had the life we had."

Margie worried most about young Glen when the family began to discuss fostering. He really wasn't on board with the idea, but Margie knew "his wheels inside that little head were turning."

Standing in the kitchen one day, he asked Margie, "Do those kids have anywhere else to go?" Margie answered that there were other foster homes out there, just not enough. (At this point, the "kids" were theoretical, not specific.)

Glen's face grew troubled. "Would they be as nice to the kids as we would?"

Take a deep breath, Margie thought. Then she responded, "Some would. Some wouldn't. Since we have room for more than one, we'd keep brothers and sisters from having to live apart."

Glen sighed. "Well, we have to. If we don't, where will they go? They need us."

Margie's voice breaks as she recalls the conversation. "That was huge because he didn't want to. But he did. Proud parent moment."

Soon Glen had three younger siblings, first as fosters, then as forever family. "I actually think it's important to keep the birth order intact, to adopt younger. Then your older ones can be role models. He could handle having a younger brother. Could he have handled suddenly having another older one? Still, everyone's different."

Glen took to his younger brother, Chad, with more enthusiasm than Margie expected, once an initial warming-up period passed. "It was huge for Chad to have two older brothers around who don't hit women, to be able to ask them questions, to find ways to divert aggression and be a man without being a guy who hits. He still has trouble with anger management, but his aggression would have been far worse had he not had two brothers. And Glen is fifteen now, and he has a great relationship with his little brother. It made him more stable, more mature."

But don't get the idea that it was all smooth sailing. One day, Margie was in the living room, waiting on Melody to get in the car, and the little girl said, "Be right there. I just have to go hit your son."

Whaaaa? Margie thought, following her into the kitchen where, sure enough, four-year-old Melody punched ten-year-old Glen on the arm. When asked outright, Glen said, yes, she'd been doing that for quite some time. Margie sat Melody down and explained that hitting was not a way to deal with anything, and asked, why was she?

"It turned out she had this kind of 'get your retaliation in first' defense-mechanism thing going on. After we talked, she quit doing it. Really quit. I asked Glen about it until he told me to cut it out, she really was done. But that brought home to me what the classes said: supervision without stopping. Watch the new kids closely when they land in your home because you don't want to deal with surprises afterward; you want to head those off."

Her oldest daughter, Natalie, also observed (and helped end) Melody's violent orientation. Sandy and Margie were in the den one evening, disagreeing over what the family should do that weekend. Melody hovered, watching, and Natalie came to stand near her. After the argument was resolved, the little girl left the room, but not before Margie caught sight of her face.

"Natalie called it. She said, 'Mom, she expected you and Dad to hit each other, didn't she?' Yes, she did. The ways they learned new things were just what they saw in front of them, the same way they learned the stuff that wasn't going to help them in life."

It was Natalie who wholeheartedly, even passionately, embraced the fostering plans her parents made. She took her younger siblings to the playground, went to kids' movies with them, and took them for neighborhood walks. Margie believes Natalie will probably foster and adopt because she internalized the idea that "it's not just about our family; it's about our society—who can we help, how we can help. I think all three of my bios are better people because of what we did. We didn't make life better for three kids; it was for six."

However, don't get the idea that fostering confers sainthood on you. Margie laughs at this concept. "People say that: how cool it is that we're doing this; we must be saints. And I crack up. Because I admit it, when we first started I thought what we were doing was so great—change the world—wonderful people, us. I thought I would feel good about it.

"In fact, most of the time with my second set of kids, I feel guilty. I'm always second-guessing myself. 'Oh, I should have hugged her, not talked at her. Oh, we shouldn't have made a punishment for that. Why did I say that?' Etcetera. Guilt: it's way more prevalent than any feel-good moments. Maybe new fosters aren't prepared for that at all. It's an iterative process."

Social worker Barbie grunts when she hears Margie's story. "I'm dealing with a young family right now. When they started going through the licensing classes, they bragged about it on Facebook. Every time they attended, they posted afterward. You could tell that they came in with that thought process. 'Everybody's gonna think this looks so good!' They wanted to post pics of the foster kids online. Hello! Bad idea!

"But they're all, 'We're doing such a great thing! We're getting so many kudos at our church! Everything's gonna be great!' And then they didn't receive the child they requested. They wanted a younger kid. Right after they got licensed, a teen became available. It wasn't a good match by their answers. But they said, 'That's okay! We'll give it a shot anyway!' It was a disaster. They had young children not used to a teenage mouth. That poor girl came back to us within a month."

Many caseworkers have watched the self-destruction of parents who exhibited "that vibe, the one that says they should be nominated for sainthood because they've done such a brave, selfless act." Dale shakes his head. "You just hope they figure it out before they break some kids' hearts. Or more, we hope they reach deep down and pull their compassion out and get with the program. They could be great parents if they get past lusting for that crown of laurels. Most of them do, but it's hard. You get a lot of accolades being a foster parent, sure, but deep down you get a lot of mistrust too. It's not a natural impulse to raise somebody else's child."

Fostering may not convey sainthood, says Margie, but it does offer a unique opportunity to alter the course of human development. "People believe foster parents change the lives of the kids they take in, and that's a good thing. But it runs deeper than that. We're changing it also for their adult future and for their kids someday, when they have their own and raise them themselves. We're trying to help them be productive members of society, to enjoy their time on earth, to change that whole bad streak into good and carry that forward, instead of the hard stuff. It's all about the kids that are coming next; if these kids have safety, security, love, their needs met, so they can become who they are instead of having to be in survival mode all the time, then they can do that for the next generation. We can change the trajectory for this subset. Granted, it's a tiny subset, but we each do what we can do."

That, says Dale, is what foster care is about. And if enough people were doing that, "it would work."

14

Look for the Sunshine, not the Rain Clouds

When you're feeling hopeless, hug your child. It's amazing how they remind us our life is always full of love.

—Pinterest quote

THE STORIES told here are a little piece of a big picture. The chaos, desperation, frustration, compassion, and hope go on. If many of the stories seem negative, it is perhaps because of the limitations of the storytelling-journalism approach. Those who don't get a chance to talk very often could say what they pleased without fear of repercussions. Or perhaps the negative stories have always been there, but not a public appetite to hear and understand them. Americans love underdogs, but we really hate to be inconvenienced. These stories are inconvenient to hear, because once comprehended, they pretty much demand a response.

Or perhaps there is a third element that Dale points out: "None of this 'be warned' stuff encompasses the thrill of making a lifetime change in a child. People can't expect every day to be glorious, but this isn't done in a vacuum. You really do get joy from the job."

By "job," Dale means parenting, not social work, yet the rewards are similar for both. In my interviews, neither group talked much about the moments of joy in recognizable ways, I thought. Dale tells me I thought wrong.

"They did. I read it. They talked about the challenges of changing lives, chipping away on a daily basis. That boy who peed in the sink? They adopted him." Amy, the honors student who had the burger meltdown, went trick-or-treating last Halloween. He ticks through other cases: the brothers reunited after a year's separation due to the diligent detail management of a social worker; the malnourished twin boys who grew into hulking second graders "blooming like sunflowers."

"See, I think readers might fall into the trap where they expect the heavens to open and a rainbow to shine down or something. That's not what this job is, and that's not parenting. It's a whole lot of daily grind, with enough stardust and rejoicing to keep you going back for more."

The moments that keep social workers going are so small and so simple that they can be easily missed by those not living inside the foster care clockworks. Beth told me a story I hadn't thought much more about until Dale delivered his "you're seeing it wrong" summation. In her first year as a social worker, she'd had an eleven-year-old boy with severe dental damage. She organized trips for dental care, including caps and partial dentures. At her annual review with her first supervisor, she expressed frustration that the boy had gone back to his family home without much hope of staying there—that he seemed personally disinterested in his own life development—and sadness at "not being able to help him."

"And my supervisor, she said, 'You did help him. You got him new teeth. You know how hard it is to get a job with bad teeth? He's going to grow up better off because of that.' And that wasn't what I was looking for, but I thought, *You know, that is a positive change.* So I learned to count the little things as maybe not so little. Who knows what changes will make what other changes happen?"

Beth told that story early in the project, and at the time I dismissed it as excusing the inability of the system overall to make positive differences. A year later, I see her point: a change like that is positive and not to be sneezed at. Take the rays of sunshine when they break through the clouds. It's not that there aren't that many of them, it's just that they're smaller than the "Aha" glory moments we want to hear about. But if we think about it, isn't much of life's fun those small, sweet moments?

The first time a child gets a Christmas present when they are ten or even eleven years old can be a wonderful thing. The first batch of cookies they make from scratch. Their first set of matching sheets, picked out themselves. These are small moments, but they are special ones.

"Think about your childhood memories. Sure, there's some big things in there, but think about all the little things that made your childhood happy. You're the product of all those little moments, and these kids, when they finally get some of those—that's a moment we celebrate. You get what I'm saying? Stop expecting the angels to sing. Be happy this kid is happy because he's got a plastic pumpkin chock-full of candy and he's with a bunch of kids his own age being a kid. That's childhood. That's winning."

Dale is looking for people who understand that parenting foster kids just might be three parts commitment, one part humor, and two parts practicality. People who say, "These kids are mine for life" and mean it—despite damaged hardwood floors, stolen money, sexualized behavior, and everything else.

He puts it this way: "When people stand at the altar and say, 'I do,' and they're looking at each other dewy-eyed, and everyone is crying, they have no idea then how many times they're going to want to undo that 'I do.' But they don't. They stick with it. Fostering is a lot like that. You go into it with no idea how changed you're going to be, how tired you're going to be, within two weeks. People don't understand, until they really see some of the examples in the classes, what kind of things they're in for. But we train them to be ready for the difficult so they can enjoy the good."

In addition to those sweet moments, there is the daily empowerment of knowing that you are a child's champion. There's a slogan in education that suggests "each one teach one." In foster care, it might be "each one protect one." When Cody told me, early in my writing, "Kids are dead last in this system, you'll see," I thought he was just being cynical ol' Cody. He wasn't.

Many of the foster parents and children I talked to described either the moment they became a protector for someone else, or the moment when they needed one who appeared (or didn't), and the course of their life altered as a result. If you're going to be a foster parent, you will have to fight for the child in front of you. You will find that at times the law helps you, and at times you will be trying to find ways to go around it. This is where the goals of social workers and foster parents diverge, and the classes don't help. Educate yourself not just about what the system tells you but about what it doesn't. Be prepared for the strangest fights you never thought you'd have in support of a child. Talk to other foster parents, and join a support group.

In fact, a support group is part of the advice foster parents offer to those interested in fostering:[1]

1. Do respite or emergency care first. The placements are quick and sometimes intense. This will let you know if you can handle long-term fostering or adoption.

2. Lock away every single thing you value enough to cry over for at least a year. It's not about trust; it's about not putting your grandmother's quilt in a place where it can get pitted against your new foster daughter. Don't let opportunity arise to have to choose between objects and people.

3. Foster and adopt below the age of the youngest birth child in your house. This avoids many complicating factors.

4. Don't try to force trust. Learn to recognize the opening signals of communication and encourage them, but don't try to force them out of the kids.

    (For example, one foster child heard me talk about a situation in which a boy and his foster mom were folding laundry. As he pulled out one of her dresses, he looked at it and said, "My dad used to make me wear—" and stopped. The mother took the dress from him and said, "Well, don't you worry. Nobody's gonna make you wear one here." I thought this was a compassionate response, but the foster child disagreed. "He was giving her an opening. She should have said, 'Made you what?' or 'Do you want to talk about it?' He was signaling. She didn't hear, and she lost a chance.")

5. Recognize that it's not just you: your whole family is fostering, and you are fostering the child's whole family. They do not sever relationships because you want them to, and it's not healthy to expect them to. Also, your parents, your siblings, and your children are now involved in this child's life. Get everyone on board before you start.

6. Have a support system. No matter how strong you think
    you are, you are going to need people you can talk to.
    People who get the things you're saying and aren't about
    judgment or advice. People who just listen.

7. Educate yourself. Take every class offered and every up-
    grade allowed, and learn about parenting, fostering, and
    the system whenever you get the chance. It all helps.

8. Go to the court dates if possible. Keep an eye on this ball,
    and don't let anything big slide past. Because it will.

9. Nobody needs a martyr. Don't give until you can't. Do
    self-care. Keep it small and simple, and be prepared to flex,
    but do it.

10. Remember the unknowns. The kids have triggers, and so
    do you. Until you learn what they are, you'll find them by
    hitting them. It's not your fault. It's not their fault. It just
    is.

11. Accept that each child is an individual person. When all
    is said and done, his life belongs to him. You can guide,
    support, love, cherish, and protect her, but you can't live
    her life for her. Don't try.

Dale laughs when I show him the list, and says, "You're describing parents
who pay attention to the things we tell them during the licensure process."
Well, yes.

15

Finale

If you're not in the arena also getting your ass kicked, I'm not interested in your feedback.

—Brene Brown

AT THE end of a year of talking to people about the system of foster care and adoption in the Coalfields, what is left to say?

Perhaps what made the biggest impression to a newbie wandering around, listening to people on the inside and watching the way things worked, was how often the system seemed to pull against itself. I expected a fair bit of darkness edging into this behind-the-curtain world of moving parts. What I didn't expect were the tensions between those who on first blush looked as though they should be allies.

Picture a triangle: on one side are the social workers, on a second wait the foster parents, and on the third sit the courts, with the bio parents moving between the DSS and the judicial sides. Even though there are instances reported here and regular occurrences elsewhere of foster families trying to work with bio families, the relationship almost never sticks. With the exception of one open adoption, at no points did I find birth and foster parents working well together for longer than six months or so. The tensions between them were palpable when conducting interviews.

I wasn't surprised that most people, inside the system or out, also took a dim view of judges and courts. Although a vocal group of child care professionals advocate that families should stay together at almost any cost, the general public tends to disagree. This is a nuanced and culturally layered debate less explored here than the frustration of foster children bouncing through the system and foster parents who want to adopt them. I urge anyone interested in the national picture of foster care to research the assistance versus removal debate, with its tough yet apt questions about directing resources toward the prevention of rather than the management of child endangerment.

More startling than attitudes toward courts and judges was to hear the kids express poor opinions of social workers overall.

"Nobody changed my life," said one. "I didn't have a champion. Just me, working through the system until I got out." Others found champions in good foster parents. Not one foster kid mentioned a social worker as standing out. This just about broke the hearts of social workers who read early drafts of this manuscript. The reasons could be many; social workers often have to say no to kids; they work behind the scenes; and so on. Suffice it to say that the social workers were not happy with what they read about the kids' attitudes toward them en masse.

By contrast, social workers talked about special kids often, the ones that got under their skin, kept them awake nights with worry—the kids they could help, the kids they tried to help, the kids who wouldn't let themselves be helped. Social workers' vitriol was reserved largely for judges, courts, and—unexpectedly, perhaps, to many of us—foster parents. Very few DSS employees of any stripe (family preservation, caseworker, social worker, what have you) complimented foster parents as a whole, although some praised a few individuals they considered exceptions to the norm.

Foster parents usually didn't want to talk about anyone or anything except their kids, but when pressed, they displayed tension between themselves and just about everyone else. While there are exceptions, foster parents as a body don't speak in ways that suggest they trust, like, or respect social workers. They think DSS is part of the problem. Their views on therapeutic care might be gentler, agency by agency, but overall, foster parents felt isolated and alone inside the bumpy, chaotic system. They didn't feel able to rely on the social workers, and they lived in terror of (and possibly in a permanent state of fury with) the courts.

Adoptive parents had more lenient views, although some said outright that they adopted so that they could get out of the crazy system of foster care overall: caseworkers, DSS, judges, and all. I wasn't expecting the system to work against itself in this way.

No matter how unintentionally, Cody and other veterans pass on a healthy skepticism of foster parents' motivations and ability to persevere, gleaned from their many years in the field. From the family's point of view, perhaps the suspicion results from how little ability any social worker has to shield the children—and by extension, their would-be shelter providers—from the bounces of court-ordered returns. Not that this is fair to the social workers, who cannot exert power the system does not give them, but fairness is not a virtue much observed in life generally. Witness the fact that social workers may be required to assist in setting up and keeping appointments for bio family visits that the foster parents see as detrimental to their charges. While the resultant ill will may not be fair, it is understandable.

That's the good side of mistrust. On the darker side, social workers may believe that families are not providing what the children need and may long for an opportunity to find better placements. Foster families with less heart and more interest in cash don't want that kind of scrutiny. Kids make false allegations against foster parents as retaliation for discipline, because they hope to force a move in order to reunite with siblings, or simply when they're angry and have no other way to lash out; or the allegations may be true, and the kids are really asking for help. Social workers have to wade through the murky waters and find out. Nothing in that remit leans toward the building of trust.

Perhaps the biggest irony of this suspicion is that foster care workers and foster care parents seem a fairly holistic group to the public, their disparate goals not always evident. Social workers and foster parents alike are perceived as saints and sinners, not people like the rest of us. Foster families are the best of humanity for taking in these sweet lost children, but they're doing it for money, whisper the crowd behind their hands. Social workers are either the saints of the modern world or the laziest individuals since sliced bread. Middle ground doesn't exist when people talk casually about foster care. It's too weird and too removed from mainstream experience for its system of moving interactive gears to show in public. Some of its governing laws are so strange, friends who read my research didn't believe the stories were real.

Having observed so many moments where those gears are grinding and spinning with no particular place to go, one has to ask, what would make things go better?

First, foremost, last, always: more stable foster parents. That would include more communal awareness of the state-sponsored foster care process in the first place, and then a deeper understanding of its myriad tricks and turns and hall of mirrors distorting so many of the essentials. Like the proverbial six blind men with their elephant, nobody (with the possible exceptions of lifers such as Dale and Karen) can see all the pieces of the foster care system like a strategic map because the system isn't designed to work together within itself.

Prospective foster parents should go into caregiving armed with a few facts that no one inside the system is eager to point out, since the facts clash with their goals, or perhaps make them look like the bad guys. The list in the previous chapter covers much of it, but not all. Perhaps the biggest overall concern is to recognize that your kids could be pulled away from you unexpectedly, yet you are first in line to adopt them if they aren't. Next, you're going to get "paid" and need to be prepared for the strange corrupting influence that money will bring to the table, even if you know you're fostering for good reasons. Per number 11 on the list, understand that no matter at what age you adopt them, these children that you pour your life and soul into are going to look for their birth parents someday, and the reasons why they will have nothing to do with you. Recognize that you're going to find a whole bunch of craziness in the system and will wind up blaming someone—parents, judges, social workers, yourself. But you'll also be somebody else's craziness, because the chaotic fostering and adoption processes involve so many silos and cross-purposes that you may never even meet the person who unwittingly destroys your world. You also may become that person to someone else and not know it. Or do it on purpose because you believe yours is the moral high ground.

The system that sets itself up to hide these facts from foster parents is ingrained in the social workers' culture of enforced positivity and salesmanship. Prospective parents need to know what they're in for. Social workers need—and from what I observed, usually want—to help foster parents enter the process with discernment. Yet they don't want to scare people away, either. Social workers also seem stymied (by many factors: the chaos of removal, regulations, timing of their workload in a specific instance, or an overall disinterest/laziness, among others) from providing essential facts that would help the parents. Last but not least, triggers are a big deal in the foster care world. With good reason.

For their part, foster parents don't always believe or accept advice from social workers. They don't agree with the legal requirements caseworkers are bound by. And while they may honor the larger reasons why regulations and citations for infractions of them are in place, no foster or adoptive parents I spoke with believed their child's caseworker should have written them up for failure to supervise (the most common citation) or any other infraction of foster parenting. It's important to have citations and rules; it was wrong to say they broke them.

Social workers are looking for people to make the world better for a child, people with no stars in their eyes, no expectations of praise, no belief that a child will love them ten minutes after arrival. Social workers may also come the closest of anyone inside the system to recognizing that the foster care world is an octopus with schizophrenia. One arm seeks to take kids away, another tries to restore them, a third wants adoptions at all costs, and a fourth is financially rewarded for avoiding adoption. With so many competing goals, and so much money fueling the process, how could there be anything but chaos? The good social workers try to stand between it and the children, but they know—oh, how they know!—that they can only soften blows more often than deflect them. Foster parents try to deflect these blows as well, and feel equally helpless. In the end, frustration just might be the signature emotion felt by those on either side of watching over children not born to them.

Foster care is one of the few programs that money is not going to help, at least not as it is currently directed. One could argue that money is in fact exacerbating the problem, both by being used within the system like a fishing lure to get kids off the books, and by attracting private agencies. Homes in Coalton are using care money to supplement personal income, but remember Dale's analysis: the economics of the region are such that people with generous hearts can't always afford to be generous. So just how did we get from there to the point at which system insiders label 30 to 70 percent of homes as in it more for the money than for the kids, what I came to call "paycheckers"? Is it judgment from those not willing to participate, unable to admit that hope comes with a price tag? Or is it an accurate assessment of the corrupting influence of the cash swirling around the children's needs? Monetary assistance is indeed morally tricky territory. Perhaps it is misdirected; Cody would certainly like to see more of it set aside to help those aging out rather than to supplement adoptions within. Nationally there is a movement to fund prevention of removals in preference to foster care.

We who advocate for the Coalfields rarely find ourselves in a position of arguing that too much funding is being thrown at a problem. Is there too much funding, not enough, or ineffective distribution? Whatever panel decides the final answer needs to include foster and adoptive parents, foster and adopted children, and caseworkers who have been there, seen that.

A better fix that has been provided regionally really has assisted with the "cued up" foster parents suggestion; foster parents need to understand more clearly that they are taking on a whole family, not just the foster children. For that and so many other reasons, foster parents need to have a support system around them, per number six on the parental list of the previous chapter. Kudos to the Coalton team that first created one at their Industry Park offices. It has brought stability and accountability to many families, and the original group has been emulated across the region.

Another fix is less feasible. Better communication between the goals of the courts, of the families, and of the social workers would be a big plus, but that's asking for the Titans to sit down and draw up mutual terms over a nice civilized cup of tea. If a fairy godmother appeared and waved her magic wand, perhaps. Short of that, this ideal world doesn't exist—in Coalton or in America. But until that happens, social workers and foster parents alike will continue to believe they are the stronger force for child advocacy as a whole, and the more invested individuals in specific situations. Sometimes they are equals, sometimes one is more invested, and sometimes neither one seems too concerned.

Foster care in Coalton is a merry-go-round of wild horses ridden by angry, frightened children, ringed by social workers who try to keep them from falling off. Behind the workers, a huge sign hangs on the central pole, the one driving the engine. The sign around which everything else rotates reads "Remember: we haven't got enough foster homes to be picky." Meanwhile, the carnival barker sets twenty-dollar bills on fire and throws them in the air, to the delight of a roaring crowd titillated by the spectacle, only too happy to bad-mouth the waste rather than enter the chaos and pluck a child off the merry-go-round.

What's shaking the walls of Coalton's fun-house maze of foster care is that lack of dedicated foster homes. Not homes where life is peachy-keen, just places that pay attention to what the kids need, who they are, and who they can become if they're allowed to concentrate on growing up instead of surviving. Homes where decent, compassionate, nonsaintly people buy kids Christmas gifts with money not taken from their care stipends. Homes that take them to McDonald's, ask how practice went after school, help with homework, enforce bedtimes. Homes that mean it when they say, "I'll always be here for you."

Part of what stops people from fostering is what they find in their own hearts. I examined again and again whether I'd be a candidate for foster parenting. Not everyone can do it. It's inconvenient and scary to think about raising someone else's children. Chaos, frustration, desperation, hope, and compassion are knotted together so tightly that you can't separate them.

Chaos, because taking a child from a home is in itself a terrifying and dangerous act. It may not be the best act society can perform—a question left alone for the most part in this work—but one that looms large nonetheless. If you do take a child away from his parents, is he going to a safer, better place more likely to feed and clothe him and make sure he has blankets on the bed? Are safety and stability going to heal the emotional wounds that his leaving rips open? That's not a yes-or-no question. This whole system needs a good shakedown on that subject, but how do you clean an airplane engine while it's flying?

Frustration, because the children will make stupid moves, like Toby, Jody, and Amy. Children make mistakes they aren't old enough to see as near-fatal inside the system. These children may be too experienced at life, but they're not self-caring in their wisdom. Savvy about some things, naïve about others, they don't respond to the normal cues, and you have to start with where they are. Which is usually some version of desperate and shutdown.

Desperation, because the kids caught inside something they can't influence yet are the objects of other people's decisions. Leaving aside the misjudgments and mistakes that one makes growing up, not having any control over one's own life can make a body pretty crazy. Ronna, Cami, and many of the others interviewed here knew at very young ages what was happening to them. They also knew they couldn't do much about it, except learn to "be good" and manipulate from within. Or to be bad and do the same.

Desperation (not to mention frustration), because the social workers who want to do good often can't because they have six homes for twenty sets of siblings. They have to choose between bad options, and that choice includes using places for which they receive public condemnation. How does one pick between a home where a child sleeps on a porch with no blanket and eats prefabricated burritos from the frozen-foods section, and a home where a child is eating well and has his own room but gets ignored emotionally, perhaps verbally abused? Desperation, because parents who can't have children would give their eyeteeth to care for some of the kids floating through the system, but if they do find one another, court-ordered yo-yoing could blow their relationship to smithereens. Parents who want to give it their all break apart after two or three slides down that yo-yo string.

Hope, because a lot of compassionate people are trying to offer stable childhoods. Rebecca and Sam. Annie and her new husband (who despite Annie's plans otherwise did start fostering again). Ronna. Margie and Sandy. With motivations ranging from (in one case) humanist to Christian to "I just don't want it to happen to anyone else," these foster and adoptive parents have stepped into the breach. Hope, because social workers are trying very hard to recruit more parents and to ensure that the nets designed to catch the rotten fish do so. Private agencies are trying to get more kids assigned to therapeutic care—not just for the money, but because they can see these children falling apart with each successive bounce.

And compassion, because despite all the craziness, many people enter foster care for good reasons. They want to give back, help a child, and be the safety, stability, and emotional engagement that young'un has been longing for. Parents and kids alike are looking for love, and many good, honest people commit for the long haul by saying, "I'm afraid, but I'm willing to learn." In the words of Beth, "How can you break something that's already smashed?"

Good question.

Unless someone like you cares a whole awful lot, nothing is going to get better. It's not.

—*Dr. Seuss*

Notes

INTRODUCTION: WELCOME TO COALTON

1. Children living with parents accounted for 490 of 496 children available for adoption in the "Coalton" district at the time of writing, according to a count from the district office. About 110,000 children are available for adoption nationwide, at least half of whom have living parents, according to the Adoption and Foster Care Analysis and Reporting System (AFCARS).

2. In fact, when this manuscript was sent to preliminary readers including social workers and educators, the feedback boiled down to "Really honest, and oh so depressing; can we get some sugar in this salt?"

3. For examples of what we're trying to avoid, please read the discussion comments of any online forum involving adoption and foster care. You can find several at adoption.com/forums.

CHAPTER 1: LOOKING FOR LOVE—AND BABIES

1. Appalachian Regional Commission and county websites.

2. Statistically, just over half of US children entering foster care will reunite with their parents in a given year. Twenty-five percent of those in care nationwide are available for adoption (AFCARS); Coalton DSS workers suggest their area's figure may be slightly lower, perhaps 20 percent.

3. Two years is technically the maximum allowed under the law.

CHAPTER 2: A DIFFERENT KIND OF LOVE THAN I WANTED

1. Nationally, 46 percent of children who enter care go to nonrelated foster homes, 29 percent to a relative, and the rest to facilities or other arrangements (AFCARS). DSS workers in Coalton suggest that the numbers in their area are almost even between relatives and nonrelatives. Very few group homes operate in Coalton, and the ones that exist are private, not state-run.

CHAPTER 3: THROUGH THE EYES OF A CHILD

1. CASA websites suggest this figure is nationwide.

CHAPTER 4: TWO REBOOT CAMPS

1. A search for nationwide statistics on how many foster children become foster parents proved fruitless; anecdotally, the number is said to rise in the urban areas of the Coalfields.

2. Stats on accusations are hard to come by, let alone verify. At least one state (Oregon) has a higher standard for proving abuse in a foster home than in a birth home. Oregon also self-reports fewer than 1 percent of its foster homes as abusive. (*Chronicle of Social Change*)

3. Multiple government sites "track" abuse; their circumvention in providing actual information is fascinating. Here is one example: https://www.childwelfare.gov/topics /systemwide/statistics/can/stat-outofhome/.

CHAPTER 5: DOING GOOD, WELL

1. An early reader of this manuscript pointed out that this is illegal.

CHAPTER 6: FOR LOVE OR MONEY

1. This is not a term social workers use. It is more common among the general public, and if a social worker is quoted using it here, he or she was likely repeating words I had been using.

2. VEMAT is the name of the system in Virginia; it is available online and shows how stipends are set.

3. Dale is closest to the estimated national average. Paycheck homes are not necessarily physically or verbally abusive, and as one can imagine, there are no reliable statistics on "paycheckers." The closest one can come to assessing manipulation of the system is when a home moves from dispassionate disinterest to neglect or abuse. National information is fragmented and hard to come by, but independent reports suggest one-third of foster homes could successfully be documented as abusive if investigated, if one includes neglectful circumstances. DSS usually reports the number of abuse cases within its own network, so state government statistics are not used here as a reliable source. For further information from third-party sources, visit https://chronicleofsocialchange.org /blogger-co-op/abuse-foster-care-denial-runs-deep/16834.

CHAPTER 7: WHAT'S LOVE GOT TO DO WITH IT?

1. To the general public—and as it is used here—"failed adoption" means a child is returned from an adoptive home to foster care. Within foster care, these returns are commonly called "disruptions," while "failed adoption" means one that did not go through in the first place, usually because children return to their parents or a relative.

2. The family has no religious affiliation or belief. "Agnostic" is a less comfortable term to Margie than "not of a religious persuasion."

CHAPTER 8: LOVE, UNDERSTANDING, AND FECAL MATTER

1. http://www.dbhds.virginia.gov/individuals-and-families/community-services-boards.

CHAPTER 9: AGING OUT

1. Nationally, about 2 percent of children who age out of foster care complete a college education: http://www.goodhousekeeping.com/life/parenting/a35860/adoption-statistics/.

2. At the time of writing, all but one community college in Virginia had such a program.

3. States vary. Sometimes they stop at eighteen, sometimes not. Visit the VEMAT website for information on the financial structure in Virginia, for one example.

4. States vary. Virginia cut its funding in 2014; this is the state Barbie is discussing.

5. LCSW Cassie supported this figure; I found no specific references online.

6. Nationally, 80 percent of the prison population consists of adults who were in the foster care system at some point during their childhood. http://www.goodhousekeeping .com/life/parenting/a35860/adoption-statistics/.

7. According to the social workers, the teacher was given a verbal warning.

8. A disruption.

9. Nationally, this statistic could be as high as one in twenty-five for teen adoptions: http:// www.today.com/parents/it-takes-more-love-what-happens-when-adoption-fails-918076.

10. One in four foster kids who age out of care becomes homeless within five years: http://www.upworthy.com/9-things-to-know-about-kids-in-foster-care-plus-an -unforgettable-view-into-their-lives.

11. Across the United States, by the age of twenty-four, just under 70 percent of girls raised in foster care will have children. (National Foster Care Coalition)

CHAPTER 10: CURSED BE THE TIES THAT BIND

1. Fostering Connections to Success and Increasing Adoptions Act of 2008 (P.L. 110–351), https:// www.childwelfare.gov/topics/systemwide/laws-policies/federal/fosteringconnections/. A similar law had been passed in 1997.

2. That's the Coalton estimate from interviews with social workers. Nationally, 54 percent of the children entering foster care had a goal of reunification set by their case workers/courts/DSS in 2014. And about 51 percent went home again within a year. The problem is that afterward, the stats count only when they leave again, not how often they go in and out. Remaining in the home for five years or more without further bounces is not counted (https://www.childwelfare.gov/pubPDFs/foster.pdf). In 2012, 2 percent of those reunited with families had died within a year, according to the Child Maltreatment Report conducted annually by the Department of Health and Human Services (https:// www.acf.hhs.gov/sites/default/files/cb/cm2012.pdf).

3. The essay compilation *Public Health in Appalachia,* edited by this author, includes an article detailing the timeline of when opioid painkillers entered the Coalfields.

4. That's the Coalfield statistic, according to several within the area, but some so-cial workers said half. Fewer than 10 percent of foster kids are recorded as seeking their parents nationally (http://statistics.adoption.com/information/adoption-statistics-birth -family-search.html), but even those who disputed 80 percent called the national assess-ment, in the words of one, "hogwash." Others used a stronger term.

CHAPTER 13: WHY PEOPLE DON'T FOSTER, AND WHY THEY DO

1. Not counting internal family adoptions, about 60 percent of adoptions nationwide are of state-sponsored foster children: http://www.pbs.org/pov/offandrunning/fact-sheet/. Good Housekeeping research, at the address in note 1 to chapter 9, puts this figure closer to 40 percent; in Coalton, nonstate adoptions are uncommon.

CHAPTER 14: LOOK FOR THE SUNSHINE, NOT THE RAIN CLOUDS

1. One foster parent had written a list when she finished fostering but decided not to publish it because she felt it would deter prospective foster parents from entering the system. This is an adaptation from several parents' editing of that list.

Additional Resources

There are thousands of adoption and foster care resources available by state and nationally, as well as via international agencies. Weeding through them can be daunting. Checking who put out the information—a state versus a private agency, an individual or a community organization—can help investigators interpret the information provided. In no particular order, here are a few I found useful as introductions to the big picture of US foster care.

Shelby Redfield Kilgore is a Korean adoptee dedicated to raising awareness about the many faces of adoption through video storytelling. Her website is Kismet at http://www.yoonmeichae.com/index.html. You can also Google her works on YouTube, Vimeo, and Facebook. She covers several different family situations, mostly in an urban environment.

ABC's popular *What Would You Do?* series set up a scene in which diners were confronted with an "in it for the money" foster parent scenario. To see what happened, visit YouTube on https://www.youtube.com /watch?v=P_7DsMJoqu8.

A Fostered Life is a YouTube channel of more than fifty videos run by Christy K. She and her husband foster children in urban Seattle, although she is from Virginia. Aimed mainly at people interested in or beginning to foster, her videos offer great insights into day-to-day home life, and sometimes the larger system in which it takes place. Christy makes videos in response to viewer questions at afosteredlife@gmail.com.

Carla the Bubblelush, also on YouTube, answers questions on Fridays from those interested in the foster care journey she and her husband took. She is in Oregon. Carla speaks openly about money (using her state's figures on nontherapeutic care) and everything else she tackles.

Mama Left Me is a novel set in the Coalfields, published via CreateSpace Independent Publishing Platform. Its author, Carol Ingram Moore, is a retired social worker and educator. Her book explores KinCare issues in cultural context.

Turning Stones: My Days and Nights with Children at Risk by Marc Parent is a memoir about a Wisconsin kid becoming a social worker in New York City. His small-town approach coupled with his sense of the limits his department and abilities face in tackling the daunting problem transcend location to provide further understanding of how frustrating, terrifying, and necessary it is to be a social worker.

Paula McLain remembered her life as a foster child with poetic detail in *Like Family: Growing Up in Other People's Houses.* Her depiction of the gaps foster children have in knowledge that most people glean from casual childhood experiences is particularly compelling.

Random Family by Adrian Nicole LeBlanc turns fieldwork into storytelling in New York City, showing how families are shuffled and reconstructed based more on economics and internal pressures than on court orders or social intervention. There is an updated version from 2016.

ReMoved (2013) is a film by Nathanael and Christina Matanick that follows the emotional journey of nine-year-old Zoe entering foster care. The opening line is, "Sometimes someone hurts you so bad, you stop hurting at all." *Remember My Story* is the follow-up film. Each is about twenty minutes long.

The national website for CASA is casaforchildren.org, but you can find specific volunteer opportunities and requirements by Googling within your state. They are always looking for volunteers. Retirees make up a large number of these and are welcomed with enthusiasm.

Molly McGrath Tierney, Director of the Department of Social Services for Baltimore, presented a 2014 TEDx talk entitled "Rethinking Foster Care." She echoes many of the ideas social workers espoused here about "save the world" foster parents and the reason why keeping children in their bio family homes provides better long-term outcomes. She also lays out the "financial incentives" Cody hinted at for agencies and individuals not to do so, in a clear and concise description. You can find her talk on YouTube or the TED channels.

If you want to investigate becoming a foster parent, Google your state and county or municipality's Department of Social Services. In some rural areas these are contracted to a private agency or run by the Community

Service Board. It is better to start with a state agency than with a private one, and word of mouth can be an ally. Avoid sites that suggest fees up front or are attached to legal offices, or that want to immediately set you up one-on-one with a "counselor," unless you are interested only in private adoption. Public information events are a good way to meet people and test the waters.